FORMIDABLE

By the same author:

The Scapegoat; The Life and Tragedy of a Fighting Admiral and Churchill's Role in his Death (2014)

The Coward? The Rise and Fall of the Silver King (2014)

www.steverdunn.com

FORMIDABLE

A True Story of Disaster and Courage

Steve R. Dunn

Book Guild Publishing

Sussex, England

First published in Great Britain in 2015 by
The Book Guild Ltd
The Werks
45 Church Road
Hove, BN3 2BE

Typesetting in Garamond by
YHT Ltd, London

Printed and bound in Great Britain by
CPI Group (UK) Ltd, Croydon, CR0 4YY

A catalogue record for this book is available from
The British Library.

ISBN 978 1 910508 15 2

To Vivienne and Emmy, for believing.

And to the memory of all the men who served in the British navy in the Great War.

Contents

Introduction

The mass slaughter on the Western Front during the First World War remains appalling, even to modern eyes jaundiced as they are by Hitler and Stalin's massacres and the potential for death inherent in nuclear weapons.

In August 1914 the British had sent the British Expeditionary Force (BEF) to France – four divisions under Sir John French to join the sixty-two French and eighty-seven German already engaged. At 160,000 men it represented virtually the entire British army. The German plan (the Schlieffen plan) was a massive right-wing-wheel through Belgium and northern France, brushing the coast and turning inland to take Paris. The French were already being badly beaten. Falling into a German trap they had launched their forces into the Ardennes and Alsace, the promise of liberating their former possessions taking precedence over logic. In the Battle of the Frontiers France lost 300,000 men in a fortnight; 27,000 were lost on one day, August 22nd; 40,000 in three days. By Christmas, France had suffered a million casualties.

The BEF was thrust into the line at Mons, in Belgium. Outnumbered three to one, 100,000 men took on the entire German First Army. They fought a running battle without rest as they retreated 170 miles, but they held on and the damage done to the German plans caused von Moltke, the German supremo, to lose his courage and turn towards Paris too soon. This exposed the German flank to a French counter attack which brought two million men into conflict. The German advance was stopped and the 'race for the sea' began – each side trying to outflank the other. A last German thrust for the sea was halted by the British at Ypres. The first Battle of Ypres began on October 20th and lasted to the middle of November. The BEF held, but the cost was awful and they were wiped out as a fighting unit. British casualties included 80,000 dead. Battalions of 1000 men were reduced to thirty. The 7th Division, 12,000 strong, lost 9,000 in eighteen days.

During the early months and years of the war the general British public had little knowledge of the scale of the killings. A combination of a gung-ho desire for glory, a patriotic fervour and press censorship meant that the losses on the Front took time to be appreciated. And of course they were also invisible; the channel hid the war from view. In time the facts would become known, the death count would rise (c. 800,000 British killed, 1.1 million if Commonwealth losses are included, and some two million wounded). We honour them in memorials and on November 11th, and rightly so.

However, in those early months of the war there were losses much nearer to home, on the seas, often close to the shore that the ships were defending. The British navy, the Senior Service, was seen by the public as Britain's strong arm and shield. As the great John Jervis, in the Napoleonic wars, said of Napoleon's putative invasion, 'I do not say, my Lords, that the French will not come, I say only that they will not come by sea'.[1] The navy, which had taken so much public money and made John Bull proud, would surely through some new Trafalgar end the German ambition in a defining sea battle.

No such battle ever occurred. But even without one the cost in men and *materiel* to the navy was high. These deaths are much less well known than those of the Western Front. By 1 January 1915 over 5,000 sailors had died at sea, many within metaphorical sight of home. The navy's sacrifices are much less well remembered than those of the armies in the field. This book is an attempt to provide a better memorial for a few of the navy's fallen.

Some positions and characters are important to the structure of the story, but are not fundamental to its telling. A brief outline of these might be of help to the reader.

The First Lord of the Admiralty is the Cabinet member with political responsibility for the navy. Between October 1911 and May 1915 the position was held by the Rt Hon Winston Churchill MP. Now rightly considered to be one of the greatest of all Britons, at the time of his tenure at the Admiralty Churchill was mistrusted by his colleagues, the press and the navy. On his appointment to the Admiralty the *Navy League Annual* stated that his arrival was not regarded with much favour; the *National Review* went one better, calling him a 'self-advertising mountebank'. The *Globe* of 21 December 1912 stated that 'the methods of Mr Churchill are wholly unfitted for the great Service of which he is the responsible head'. To many of his colleagues he was 'a maverick, widely viewed as a spoilt and bumptious child'.[2] Prime Minster Asquith had sent him to the Admiralty to reduce the costs of the navy and form a Naval War Staff. He succeeded in the latter but had the opposite effect on the former, for in March 1914 the highest naval estimates ever were announced, £50 million (around £4,800 million today).

The First Sea Lord was the executive head of the navy and responsible for strategy in time of war. He was always a senior naval officer. Successive First Sea Lords under Churchill found him anxious to hold the levers of power himself in a day-to-day fashion, which caused much friction, considerable confusion and poor decision making. At the outbreak of war the First Sea Lord was Admiral Prince Louis of Battenberg but, under the triple pressures of Churchill's interference, a press campaign against him given his Teutonic birth, and gout, he had a nervous collapse and resigned at the end of October.

Battenberg was replaced by Admiral Sir John (Jackie) Fisher. Fisher (Admiral of the Fleet Baron Fisher of Kilverstone) was the man who revolutionised the British navy in the early 1900s, dragging it protesting and screaming from the eighteenth to the early twentieth century while First Sea Lord from 1904 to 1910. He was a phenomenon; volcanic in temper, Old Testament in expression, a compulsive dancer, a man who loved and hated with a vengeance. Out of office Fisher befriended Churchill and became his *eminence grise* when the latter took over at the Admiralty. After Battenberg's demise Fisher returned as First Sea Lord, aged 73, for nine tumultuous months until he resigned again in May 1915, frustrated by Churchill's interference.

Admiral Sir John Jellicoe commanded the British Grand Fleet, based (eventually) at Scapa Flow. He had been parachuted into command by Churchill (probably at Fisher's behind-the-scenes urging) at the outbreak of war, replacing Admiral Sir George Callaghan and much against Jellicoe's own wishes. Jellicoe, like Fisher whose protégé he was, was obsessed by the threat to his fleet created by the recent development of the submarine and mines, and his detailed battle orders were conservative and preoccupied with avoiding the risk of submarine attack. Indeed, Jellicoe's fear of submarines was such that at one point he moved the Grand Fleet out of the North Sea (a considerable victory for the Germans had they but known it) and into Loch Swilly in Ireland. A centraliser, control freak and poor delegator, he remained in command of the Grand Fleet until appointed First Sea Lord in late 1916.

The man responsible for naval dispositions at the outbreak of war was the chief of staff, Vice-Admiral Doveton Sturdee. He held the post until the end of October when he was replaced on Fisher's arrival.

The prime minister on the outbreak of war was H.H. Asquith, who had held the post since April 1908. Scruffy, donnish, a heavy drinker (known to some as 'the Aged Squiff') he had the effortless sense of superiority of a Balliol man. Leading the Liberals he had been elected on a 'reformist' ticket, specifically to spend less on Britain's defence and more on social programmes, and in 1910 he narrowly achieved a majority in parliament defending the 'people's budget' which was intended to tax the rich in order to introduce welfare for the poor. In this he was somewhat stymied by the naval 'arms race' with Germany that was to be a contributory factor to the outbreak of hostilities. As prime minister he was Churchill's sponsor at the Admiralty but he did not attract the full respect of his colleagues. They subsequently depicted Asquith as a vacillating prime minister, overwhelmed by life and death decisions on a daily basis, barely able to handle the multitude of issues requiring his attention, and at best acting as a facilitator through whom men of more drive and ambition made the big decisions.

She was a ship

And the sea gave up the dead that were in it.
(Revelations 20:13)

She was a ship, but is now a tomb. A hecatomb. The last resting place for nearly 600 men and boys,* their mortal remains held in and around the rusting, rotting iron hull. She lies 200 feet beneath the surface of the English Channel, off the Jurassic Coast, Portland and the great arc of Lyme Bay. She is completely upside down. One huge bronze propeller, including its shaft, rests on the seabed close by. The other has been ripped off by some illegal salvage operation. Her secondary guns can still be seen in their casements, crushed against the sea bottom, and the huge 12-inch forward armament is visible beneath the upturned hull. Between the inverted bridge and the forward turret there is a rent in the hull some nineteen feet wide and almost cutting her in two. Fish swim in and out through it. Men could too, if she had not been designated a war grave.

She is tomb to old and young, officer and seaman, Royal Marine and stoker. The sea does not discriminate in death.

---

*There are conflicting numbers given for the total dead and survivors. Naval-history.net, which is based on primary sources, gives 204 survivors. Some other online sources give 233. However, Corbett, in the official navy history of the war (*History of the Great War*, Sir Julian Corbett) gives 197 survivors out of a total crew of 780, meaning 583 dead. That is the figure that will be used in this book.

She was once beautiful, the pride of the navy, but she got old, was pensioned off, and was then dragged out of retirement for the Kaiser's War, to die with her crew. She was formidable, HMS *Formidable*. Now she is just a wreck.

Wrecks are not unusual off that stormy coast. High seas, strong winds and an unpredictable shore line have trapped many a luckless mariner. At Portland, with its rocky coastline on its western side culminating at the Bill, several currents meet in the notorious Portland Race and make for some of the most dangerous conditions around the coastline of England. Further round the point lies the hidden Shambles, a sand and shingle bank just ten feet below the surface of the water at low tide. There is an abundance of wrecks and a tradition of wrecking. Indeed, the sea has claimed so many lives over the centuries that the local churchyards have many communal graves or memorials for the victims. Often the poor souls were just buried on the beach where the tide had thrown them up. The poet William Wordsworth lost his brother John there when the *Earl of Abergavenny* sank in 1805. She was a 1,200-ton East Indiaman en route to Bengal, but she sank on February 5th and took 261 lives with her.

Ten years earlier no fewer than six ships in Admiral Christian's fleet, heading for the West Indies to confront Napoleon's France, were lost. Some 300 or so died that day. The women and officers of rank (if it could be established) were buried in Wyke Regis churchyard where there is now a memorial tablet. The rest had a common grave on the beach. Those who survived the sea received little in the way of assistance from the locals who were busy with plundering the wrecks.

On 11 September 1877 the 1,210-ton iron ship *Avalanche* left London bound for Wellington, New Zealand, carrying sixty-three emigrants with a crew of forty-three under the command of Captain Williams. A force eight gale was blowing and there was driving rain. The seas were high and very rough. Sailing nearby was a wooden ship, the *Forest*, bound for New York and carrying a crew of twenty-one men. It was a stormy dark night, and the two ships' crews saw each other only when it was too late to avoid a collision. The *Forest* struck the middle of the *Avalanche*, rebounded and struck again, almost cutting her in two. The *Avalanche* sank straight away with the loss of 103 lives. Only twelve men survived from both ships, one of whom was the captain of the *Forest*. The responsibility for burial of the bodies, which were being washed ashore by the tide, lay with the local parish councils. They were loath to spend money on such low-class flotsam and much publicity ensued at the treatment of the dead. *The Times* thundered in outrage and the friends and relatives of those lost in the tragedy launched an appeal fund. Contributions poured in from all over England as well as New Zealand and Australia. The appeal raised sufficient funds to purchase a site and erect a memorial chapel over-looking the scene of the disaster. It was dedicated to St. Andrew and opened in 1879.

There are thought to be over a thousand wrecks along the Dorset coast; *Formidable* was in good company as she settled on the sea bed on 1 January 1915. But how did she come to be there? What concatenation of circumstances took the ship and its crew to their doom?

This book is the story of the loss of HMS *Formidable*. But it is also the story of those who survived, of courage, heroism, political 'spin', of those left behind, of consequences, and of those who might be said to be the cause of the loss, of stupidity, irresponsibility and culpability. And it is also the story of two dogs.

Part I

Tragedy

If you can meet with triumph and disaster
And treat those two imposters both the same
(Rudyard Kipling, If)

1

The Big Ship

They are grander things than all the art of towns;
Their tests are tempests and the sea that drowns.
They are my country's line, her great art done
By strong brains labouring on the thought unwon.
They mark our passage as a race of men—
Earth will not see such ships as those again.

(John Masefield, Ships)

She was born in Portsmouth, at the navy's own dockyard, on 17 November 1898 and christened by Lady Lucy Hicks-Beach, wife of the Chancellor of the Exchequer, 'Black Michael'. The British Mutoscope and Biograph Company filmed her launch, silently and in black and white. Construction work was completed by 1901, but problems with the contractors building her machinery (who went into liquidation) and engines (strikes at the engineering shops) delayed her coming out. It was only three years later that she finally entered commission as His Majesty's battleship *Formidable*, the fourth vessel to carry the name. The first, an 80-gun third rate, was captured from the French at the Battle of Quiberon Bay. Launched as the *Formidable* by the French she became HMS *Formidable*. The second, launched in 1777, was a 90-gun second rate which fought at the Battle of the Saintes as

Admiral Rodney's flagship. And in 1825 an 84-gun second rate took the name.

The fourth *Formidable* had been ordered as part of the 1897 naval estimates and programme as the lead ship of a class of three. At the time of her design she was one of the most powerful battleships in Europe, but given the delays in her commissioning she was already looking somewhat elderly when she finally emerged into the public view. Displacing over 15,000 tons and armed with four 40 calibre 12-inch guns and twelve 6-inch quickfirers, she was considered under-gunned for her size and by the time of her final completion had already been overtaken by the more heavily armed and faster King Edward VII class of battleships. Home to 780 crew – 810 if an admiral sailed on board – she was considered a good steamer, 'very handy ships, answer to the least touch of the helm'.[1] By the time she entered service the building cost was £1 million (about £103 million in today's money).

The publisher George Newnes commissioned the famous British maritime painter Charles Dixon to paint her in 1901 for his book *British Bulwarks*, containing forty-eight chromolithographs of the latest British warships. The painter depicts her in Plymouth Sound in full cry and with a red-sailed fishing smack in the foreground, an augury of things to come. Given the delays in her construction and commissioning, Dixon must have painted her mainly from his fertile imagination.

Finally commissioned under Captain Alexander W. Chisholm-Batten, *Formidable* sailed to join the Mediterranean Fleet in late 1903 (in November 1903 the *Navy and Army Illustrated* magazine headlined 'A Formidable Ship for the Med') under Captain Thomas P. Walker, to serve with the flag of the commander in chief Admiral Sir Compton Domville and his successor in 1905 Admiral Lord Charles Beresford.

The Mediterranean Fleet was Britain's premier command, based at Malta, the cynosure of everything that the navy valued and the repository of its finest ships. Resplendent in her painted finery, *Formidable* took her place with the fleet, although not for very long. Soon after arrival she went into dock for a refit which lasted until April 1905, but not before she was able to demonstrate the capabilities of her crew. In 1904, in a competition to investigate how rapidly submerged tubes could be fired four times sequentially, commencing with the tube loaded and the bar out, the ship's crew had been able to achieve a time of 1 minute 48 seconds, later improved to 1 minute 31 seconds. This compared very favourably to the typical timing of 2 minutes and 30 seconds. For a battleship her performance was very creditable.

Like any lady of note she had her portrait painted under the cerulean blue skies of the Med. Antonio de Simone, a well-known Italian marine painter, caught her in the Bay of Naples in 1905, in a painting that shows her dressed in her Mediterranean glory, black hull, white upper works, yellow funnels, a stately mistress of the waves (in 2005 Christies sold the painting for £576).

Malta was a society hub, a home away from home for the officers at least, a place where they could enjoy the same comforts and *divertissements* that, as minor aristocracy or landed gentry, they were used to in England, only at a lower cost. The social life was superb. Admiral C.C. Penrose Fitzgerald, writing in his autobiography of his service in the Med in 1889, emphasised it:

> Very good opera companies used to come to Malta for the winter months ... then, it was extremely cheap – two-and-six for a stall and boxes in proportion. Several stars, including Albani, made their debut at the Malta Opera House. There were balls, parties, picnics, polo, gymkhanas, and golf. Many of the officers of the Mediterranean squadron got their wives out from England for three or four of the winter months, and as these frequently brought with them other ladies, there were plenty of dances, riding picnics, and other innocent relaxations from the stern

routine of naval discipline. The great event of the season was the fancy-dress ball at the Governor's palace. The various and picturesque costumes of the East were always well represented.[2]

It was also not uncommon for unescorted women to visit Malta. An annual 'fishing fleet' of marriageable ladies would arrive at the island every autumn hoping for romance (or more) with the military, and especially naval, unwed (or wed!) officer population. They would stay for the 'season' and return to England in the spring.

Meanwhile, the fleet cruised around the Med, its programme mainly social and its practices largely based around complex and centralised 'evolutions' – manoeuvres. These choreographed routines were like an army parade ground display and bore little or no resemblance to the likely needs of a shooting war. When ashore, officers could enjoy dinner parties, fancy dress balls, shooting, regattas, tennis parties, golf, cricket; and if you had the financial resources, polo and horse racing. Many played tennis and golf regularly. Generations of future flag officers grew up in this comfortable environment. Military 'bull' was the rule, a smart and clean ship the route to promotion, following orders and 'fitting in' socially the most important aspect of behaviour.

All this social whirl hid an inconvenient truth. *Formidable* and her sister vessels were built for the wrong type of war and, further, were condemned to obsolescence by a revolutionary type of battleship in 1906. British naval doctrine at the time of her birth was that ships would fight in lines, as in Nelson's time, engaging at close range, using their larger guns to 'fix' and crack the hulls of her enemy and pouring in a high volume of shells from the smaller quickfirers at close range. This had been the doctrine in the time of Trafalgar, it had been successful then and the navy saw no real need to do anything different.

But the world changed around them. First, heavy guns got

bigger and longer-ranged. Ships became faster and more manoeuvrable. The torpedo, cheap and easy to carry as a 'stand-off' weapon by small, fast ships (torpedo boats and submarines), could threaten battleships from range. It became clear to some (but by no means all) naval officers that battles would be fought at longer range, which meant *Formidable*'s arsenal of quick-firing 6-inch guns could neither reach nor harm and her 12-inch rifles would be difficult to register accurately and deliver too low a weight of shell.

Second, Admiral Sir John Fisher, the revolutionary British First Sea Lord and head of the navy between 1904 and 1910, drove into service a fast, well-armoured, all-big-gun battleship, HMS *Dreadnought*, which – with its ten 12-inch heavy guns and minor secondary armament – was clearly able to out-fight and out-shoot any other battleship in any nation's navy, including the British one. *Formidable* and her sisters were immediately and doubly out of date. All navies began to build dreadnought types and a world-wide naval race was on, which soon narrowed into one primarily between Britain and Germany.

Once a blushing debutante, *Formidable* was now an old wallflower and in April 1908 she returned to England to join the Channel Fleet, subsequently paying off at Chatham in April 1909 to undergo another refit at Chatham Royal Dockyard.

The tactical deployment of ships like *Formidable* and other so-called 'pre-dreadnoughts' now became a subject of debate and a political football. Politicians wanted to count them in the fleet as fully operational battleships, capable of taking their place in the line of battle and contributing to the 'two power standard' (Britain's battle fleet to equate to the sum of the next two biggest). Many sailors disagreed, believing that such ships would have a very limited life if exposed in a battle with fully fledged dreadnought-type vessels. Fisher in particular thought their utility limited and wanted to pay many off, to free money and men for new ships; but he was prevented in this by the politicians who were frightened of both the cost and the public reaction. His solution was to create the concept of a 'Second Fleet' and 'nucleus crews'.

The Second Fleet was effectively a naval reserve, ships that Fisher no longer wanted in the line of battle but for which there might be a need in time of war, and which could be counted in the total numbers of the fleet. They were 'retired' to port where they were kept ticking over by a reduced crew of about 60% of the required complement; in time of war or for exercises with the main fleet the crew could quickly be brought up to strength by drafting men from the nearby naval barracks, reservists and boys in training. This was the status to which *Formidable* was reduced in 1912, as part of the Fifth Battle Squadron, Second Fleet (which was head-quartered at the Nore), and under the command of Captain Philip Nelson-Ward. Here she gently mouldered, Captain Ward no doubt doing his best to keep her smart as she swung on her anchor cables until he was replaced by Captain Drury St Aubyn-Wake in December.

Not that many people were fooled. An article in the *Daily Telegraph* summed up the situation nicely. 'This is the vital point to bear in mind. We are relying largely on obsolescent ships and in a comparatively short period only dreadnoughts among armoured ships will count. Owing to the obsolescence of the British battleships and armoured cruisers our strength is now steadily declining year on year.'[3]

Throughout 1913 tensions built in Europe. War clouds gathered. In Germany, France, Austro-Hungary, Russia, Britain and Serbia politicians and military men lurched unseeing towards total war, until in July 1914 the echo of an assassin's gun touched off the powder keg which consumed the world.

The whole of the navy, the First, Second and Third Fleets, had been assembled for a test mobilisation and exercises over a period of two weeks. Now it was intended to return to peacetime status and decommission the Reserve Fleet once more, and on the weekend of 25-27 July the fleet was planned to disperse following the completion of the manoeuvres. With Churchill away from his office at the seaside, building sandcastles with his wife and children, Battenberg, First Sea Lord, issued the instruction 'no ship to leave harbour until further orders' to the CinC Home Fleet (the famous signal 'stand the fleet fast', for which Churchill later tried to take credit, despite having been out of communication at the time of its issue).

This signal had the effect of ensuring that the ships of the Reserve Fleet were crewed in large part by coastguardsmen (known to the navy as 'Gobbies', naval ratings who had completed so many years in the fleet, and then went on to the reserve, with a liability for recall in time of war, and for annual exercises), boys, fishermen, enthusiastic volunteer sailors and trainees. These were men who had expected to be back at their jobs after two weeks of manoeuvres and training. Men who had not expected to go to war. In *Formidable*'s case this meant many men from Chatham and the surrounding areas.

Without such reservists and volunteers the navy could not have functioned effectively, for its strength in August 1914 stood at only 147,667 men. The order for full naval mobilisation had finally gone out on 2 August and those not already detained on their ships by the 'stand the fleet fast' signal were hurriedly called up. In Hull and Grimsby, at the East Anglian fishing ports, in the fishing communities of the south west, thousands of reservists were called up by telegram, delivery boys or policemen knocking on their doors. In Brixham nearly every family was affected by mobilisation and the town's annual regatta was abandoned. Men were commanded to report to the Customs House on the quay and depart for the naval barracks at Devonport. The cottage hospital nurses turned out to cheer them off and the chairman of the Urban District Council presided over the singing of the National Anthem at the railway station. In Looe, Cornwall, the men mustered on the quay and were marched to the railway station. In Falmouth the call up was announced by the Town Crier. The navy girded its loins. Mobilisation of the reserves added 27,395 Royal Fleet Reservists, 13,510 Royal Naval Reserve, 2,345 Royal Navy Volunteer Reserve, and 6,970 retired officers and pensioners who stepped forward once more for duty.[4] (One of the latter was Ex-Chief Gunner Israel Harding VC who had retired from the navy in 1885 but returned to the colours at the outbreak of war. Although aged over 80 he served in minesweepers until a mine blew up under his ship, breaking his left leg.) Without these part-time sailors, there would have been a very limited navy.

Like all his peers, Captain Wake had received the 'preparations for war' telegram on 27 July and the old lady under his command was brought back from her docile retirement. She once again raised steam in her boilers, took on ammunition, exercised the turret mechanisms and went to war. Not for her the glory of the Grand Fleet, streaking up the east coast of Britain to seek a safe battle station in the far north, shutting off the northern end of the North Sea and awaiting the appearance of the German fleet for the long-awaited and sought-after 'New Trafalgar'. Instead, the old lady and her spinster sisters in the Fifth Battle Squadron, now based at Portland, were sent to escort the British Expeditionary Force to France during August and then to perform the same service for the Portsmouth Royal Marines Battalion to Ostend on the 25th.

And on September 2nd Arthur Noel Loxley joined as her new Captain with his Airedale terrier, Bruce.

2

The Captain

They that go down to the sea in ships, that do business in great waters
(Psalms 107;23)

The Loxley family had deep roots in the Hertfordshire countryside, having held the Manor of Norcott, in Northchurch, Berkhampstead through the distaff side since the seventeenth century, and residing in Norcott Court. Held first by Thomas Smart and then, from 1709, by his widow Tabitha, the estate passed through two more Thomases to William Smart, who died in 1837, leaving the estate to his daughter Elizabeth. She had married John Loxley, but was widowed by the time of her inheritance and on her death in 1887 the estate passed to her son, another John, who was a partner in the law firm Loxley and Morley in London. In 1845 John had married Emily Augusta, a niece of the poet Lord Byron whose cousin was her mother. They had one child, Arthur Smart Loxley, born in 1847. No expense was spared on young Arthur's education and he attended Radley College and Exeter College, Oxford before taking clerical orders. It might be that old John was a man who favoured education, for he founded the Northchurch village school in 1864 from his own funds.

After his ordination Arthur Smart Loxley became curate of All Saints Lamport in Northamptonshire. The living was in the gift of Sir Charles Edmund Isham, 10th Baronet, of Lamport Hall (who was a keen gardener and is credited with introducing the garden gnome into England). The Isham family had held the living of All Saints since 1729 and always kept it in 'the family'. At the time of Arthur's curacy, the rector was Robert Isham, cousin to Charles, and he employed the Reverend Loxley as his curate.

In 1873 Arthur married Alice Mary Duncombe of Hatton at Stone, another Hertfordshire village some thirty miles away from Northchurch. She was the daughter of the local rector but the Duncombe family also had deep roots in Northchurch, having been long-term residents and owners of the Hall in the eighteenth century. The two families undoubtedly knew each other. A year after the marriage Alice was delivered of the first of five children, a baby boy, born on All Hallows Eve and christened Arthur Noel.

Shortly afterwards, Arthur Smart Loxley moved his family back to the ancestral home and took over the curacy of the local church of St Mary's. The advowson of the church was held by the Prince of Wales as Duke of Cornwall; but the rector for fifty years from 1830 until his death in 1880, and who paid for a curate – Loxley – to stand in for him, was Sir John Hobart Culme Seymour, 2nd Baronet Seymour and father to the extremely famous Victorian Admiral Sir Michael Culme Seymour who had been born in nearby Berkhampstead in 1836. Sir Michael, who finished his career as CinC Portsmouth, was renowned as a ship handler and had been a previous CinC of the Mediterranean Fleet, Britain's prize command of the era.

In time Arthur Smart Loxley became a minor canon of

Bristol cathedral* and gained his own preferment, becoming Vicar of Fairford, Gloucestershire. The young Noel (as he liked to be called) was sent to be educated at Eton College, demonstrating that the family had wealth that did not depend on a clergyman's stipend. Meanwhile, on his inheritance Noel's grandfather John had knocked down the old seventeenth-century house (with the exception of the Georgian dovecote) and built a brand new, half-timbered Victorian mansion befitting, as he no doubt thought, his new exalted station in life.

But in 1888 Noel's father died, aged only 41, and the 14-year-old lad was despatched to the Royal Navy training ship HMS *Britannia*. The Seymour influence might well have had a bearing on the choice of career for young Noel, and there were naval antecedents in his grandmother's family too, the poet's cousin and grandfather having been admirals.

Britannia was probably an experience not unlike that of the boarding school Noel had just left. Fagging and bullying were rife, the environment was exclusively male and Spartan, discipline was fierce, education pedagogic. Athletic skills (especially rowing, hunting, cricket) were prized, and good connections and social skills valued above intelligence.

The ship had been built in 1860 as HMS *Prince of Wales* and renamed in 1869 when she was converted into a training ship (and she continued in that role until 1905 when she was replaced by a shore-based college designed by Sir Aston Webb). She was a hulk, moored at Dartmouth, with only her foremast remaining of the original full set of sails and masts. Two terms of cadets were accepted each year and the

---

*A canon is a member of the chapter of (for the most part) priests, headed by a dean, which is responsible for administering a cathedral or certain other churches that are styled collegiate churches. The dean and chapter are the formal body that has legal responsibility for the cathedral and for electing the (arch)bishop. Minor canons are those clergy who are members of the cathedral's establishment and take part in the daily services but are not part of the formal chapter. These are generally more junior clergy, who in a parish church would be serving a curacy.

education lasted for two years, after which cadets would qualify (or not) as midshipmen and pass on to a seagoing ship. Admittance was by nomination or exam and the fees were £35 a term.

The curriculum was divided into three parts – seamanship, study, and out-study. Seamanship aimed to cover practical sailing sea lore and signalling; study gave the young cadets the chance to learn mathematics and navigation; out-study focused on French and drawing (both very practical: France was our oldest enemy and an ability to draw maps and visualisations was of practical use).

Much emphasis was placed on sports, especially sailing and boxing, and the ability to shin up and down masts and dress yards was much prized (this despite the fact that in the years while Loxley was at *Britannia* the navy commissioned the 'Royal Sovereign' class of battleship, the largest and fastest ships of their time, 13.5-inch gunned, all steam powered, and had been building such ships since the 'Devastation' class of 1869). Physical attributes were the more likely to gain a cadet respect, while doing too well in the mathematical subjects could be injurious to one's reputation.

Indeed it could be positively deleterious to one's accept-ability to perform too well in a scholastic manner. It was not necessary, or even desirable, to be academically gifted in order to progress in the Victorian navy. Cleverness was looked at somewhat askance and academic study was not particularly encouraged. A 'three-oner' – a man who obtained first-class passes at his Seamanship Board, Royal Naval College and Excellent (for gunnery) – was suspect and 'three-oners' were held in contempt by many in the navy as being 'too clever by half'. Fitting in socially and coming from the 'right' background was much more important. Noel Loxley's later career would show that he might not have fitted this mould.

Passing out as a midshipman in 1890 he was briefly posted to the Channel Squadron before being shipped far overseas to

HMS *Warspite*, Flagship of the Pacific Fleet based at Esqui-
malt, British Columbia, an assignment that would last for the
next five years. During this time he made steady progress,
being appointed Sub-Lieutenant in April 1894 (having sat
an exam and been passed by a panel of four captains)
and Lieutenant in April 1895. Progression was in part exam-
ination-based and Loxley's achievements in this regard
marked him out as unlike the archetype. On passing to Sub-
Lieutenant he had received a first-class pass in Seamanship. In
1894 he gained part 1 of his Lieutenant's exam with a second
but part 2 with a first-class pass. In 1895 he achieved a first-
class pass in Gunnery, a first in Pilotage (part I) and a first
again in Pilotage (part 2). He was a three-oner; a navy 'brain'.

Somewhere along the way he contracted malaria and this
would never leave him, causing him to be hospitalised at the
navy's own Haslar Hospital on his return from the Pacific and
at least one of his subsequent captains to remark 'strongly
recommend, liable to short attacks of malaria'.[1] He also
returned as a man of property, for during his service abroad
his grandfather had died (in 1892) and left him the Manor of
Norcott and the new house thereon, Norcott Court which
was only 4 years old. Loxley was thus assured of an income
for life.

Noel Loxley's captains clearly rated him. His 'report card'
for the time contains such comments as 'good physique, v.
zealous and intelligent' and 'recommend for advancement'.[2]
He was making his mark.

With no wars to fight at sea, many naval officers sought
battle ashore and Loxley was no exception. In 1897 he joined
a British punitive expeditionary force led by Admiral Sir Harry
Rawson in response to the defeat of a previous British-led
invasion force under Acting Consul General James Philips
(which had left all but two men dead). Rawson's troops
captured, burned and looted Benin City, dethroned the king,
and brought to an end the west African kingdom of Benin.

Loxley received the East and West Africa medal with 'Benin 1897' clasp for his pains.

In 1900, while serving in the Home Fleet, he married Gladys Maude Brooke-Hunt. Gladys, who was 17 when she married the 26-year-old Noel, was the daughter of Arthur Ernest Brooke-Hunt, born in Peers Court, Dursley. Harrow educated, a graduate of Trinity College Cambridge and The Royal Agricultural College, Cirencester, Arthur held the position of Inspector of Agricultural Education for the Board of Agriculture. The family were landed gentry, part owners of the advowson and benefice of Dinas (which they were to sell in 1909) and similar in background to the Loxleys. Arthur had married Gertrude Mabel Calvarly and sired two children, Gladys and a much younger boy, Robert.

After ten years as a lieutenant and successful completion of the 'Senior Staff Course' course at HMS *Excellent*, Loxley was promoted to Commander on 1 January 1905 – a year no doubt made doubly joyous by the birth of his son Peter in March. Appointed to the newly built armoured cruiser *Hampshire* he served under Captain Robert Arbuthnot (who, when asked by First Sea Lord Jackie Fisher what ship he would like, replied that as he had played football and cricket for the county he would like the *Hampshire*). Arbuthnot was a martinet and hard case who must have been a very demanding taskmaster. Nonetheless, Captain Arbuthnot commented of Loxley, 'very smart and gives orders well, good judgement and manners, strongly recommend; sings and acts well'.[3]

Leaving *Hampshire* after two years via the War College course, Loxley became Staff Commander to the Admiral commanding the 2nd Division of the Home Fleet, first under Sir Archibald Berkley-Milne and then Sir George Callaghan. Both rated him, Callaghan recommending him for promotion in 1910 and 1911. Milne, however, was to become something of a patron and was to repeatedly recommend Loxley for advancement. Some of Milne's comments make interesting reading: 'very zealous, hardworking, painstaking. Strongly recommend' (while still a lieutenant on *Camperdown* in 1900), 'recommend for promotion, zealous, attentive, painstaking officer, has been of invaluable assistance to me' (1909), 'recommended' (1910), 'a very zealous and reliable officer, vg gunnery and exceptional knowledge of the service. Excellent Captain of ship' (1914).[4]

Promoted captain in 1911 (on the occasion of the coronation of King George V), Loxley was sent on the staff college 'war course' before being assigned to the new *Orion* class dreadnought HMS *Thunderer*, not as ship's captain but to work on the new 'director firing' trials, examining the impact on the ship's gunnery of coordinated central laying and firing of the main guns. *Thunderer* was fitted with the Dreyer fire-control table designed by Frederic Charles Dreyer, which was a proto-computer. Loxley's assignment was to test Percy Scott's new director firing system which made *Thunderer* top-shooting ship in the 1912 trials, when she delivered over six times the hits of her sister ship in just three and a half minutes. Loxley's gunnery knowledge clearly stood him in good stead and the Admiralty expressed their 'appreciation of care and trouble taken in connexion with this important subject'.[5]

But then on 5 November 1912 this newly appointed captain, with no previous command experience, was assigned to the Mediterranean Fleet as Flag Captain to Sir Archibald Berkley Milne, Admiral Commanding, seemingly his biggest fan. This was a plum appointment and it is inconceivable that he would have got it except by Milne's special request. Who, then, was Milne and why did he champion Loxley?

Berkley Milne was the son of an admiral and baronet who became First Naval Lord under both Gladstone and Disraeli, and also grandson of another admiral. In appearance Milne was affected, sporting a non-regulation stiff turned-down collar and bow tie, a white, trimmed beard and luxuriant black moustache. He was a snob of the worst kind. Once his sleeve was brushed by a passing seaman; Milne took out his handkerchief, flicked some imagined dirt from his sleeve with it and threw the contaminated linen over the side. He was also one of those admirals who owed their position to royal influence rather than ability.

After service in the Zulu war as an ADC to Lord Chelmsford, and escaping the massacre at Isandlwana, Milne rose to the rank of captain in the navy before accepting the post of captain of HM Yacht *Osborne*, a post usually held by a commander, reasoning that exposure to royalty offered him better hopes of promotion. Such posts were often seen as mixed blessings, for they lacked any martial qualities, but Milne loved the ceremony and obsessive spit and polish of service in the Royal Squadron and went on to command the royal yachts from 1903 to 1905. He became good friends with King Edward VII and, especially, Queen Alexandra who nicknamed him 'Arky-Barky', an appellation that soon got round the fleet to humorous effect. A fellow officer asserted that Milne's hobbies were collecting rare orchids and entertaining royal ladies. Never an intellect (he is recorded as saying 'they don't pay me to think, they pay me to be an admiral')[6] and lacking any combat experience, he was nonetheless promoted through royal influence to flag rank. In 1912 Winston Churchill, First Lord of the Admiralty and under pressure from George V, made him Admiral Commanding the Mediterranean Fleet. It was not a well-received appointment in many parts of the navy.

Does Milne's liking for Loxley say anything of the latter's character? We can see an intelligent man in the record (Milne was not), fastidious and painstaking with a great knowledge of, and respect for, the navy, a hard worker; and perhaps a man who, from lack of seniority, would defer to Milne's authority. This latter characteristic would appeal to Milne but had in it the seeds of future failure.

Milne's flagship was HMS *Inflexible*. Launched in 1907 she was a battlecruiser, one of Jackie Fisher's 'greyhounds of the fleet', fast, modern, heavily armed, all big guns, designed to overwhelm lesser vessels and fast enough to evade bigger ones. It was a prize command for any captain and especially an inexperienced one.

But disaster lurked. At the outbreak of war Milne and his number two, Rear Admiral Ernest Troubridge, commanding the 1st Cruiser Squadron, had a number of missions to fulfil, not the least of which was to prevent the modern German battlecruiser *Goeben* (accompanied by the light cruiser *Breslau*) from escaping. After a series of tactical moves and mischances, the *Goeben* began a run for Constantinople with the mission of becoming part of the Turkish navy and catalysing Turkey's entry into the war on the German side. On August 7th Troubridge found himself in a position to stop them. His four armoured cruisers together packed a broadside of 8,680 pounds compared to the 8,272 of the *Goeben*. Despite his numerical superiority in ships and the ability to divide *Goeben*'s fire, Troubridge allowed himself to be persuaded not to fix and engage the *Goeben* and she made good her escape to Constantinople.

The escape was regarded by the public and the Admiralty as a great disaster, helping to bring Turkey into the war on the German side. Milne and Troubridge were vilified, the latter being court martialled. Milne was recalled to England, told to haul down his flag and never given another appointment on sea or land. Three weeks after the event Loxley was also recalled, on August 28th, and a week later he was posted to the ageing *Formidable*.

By any analysis this was a diminution of responsibility. *Inflexible* was one of Fisher's first 'greyhounds of the sea'. Heavily armed, fast, able to catch and kill anything that was of weaker armament, they could also outstrip those vessels that might outshoot them. Launched in 1907, she was still a prime command and carried an armament of eight 12-inch guns at a speed of 26.5 knots compared to *Formidable*'s four 12-inch guns and 18 knots.

Had Loxley too been blamed by implication for the disaster of the *Goeben*? As flag-captain to Milne he could have been expected to offer advice to further decision making, although it is possible that Milne chose him for the opposite reason. Whatever the case, Loxley retuned to the UK from a prime command to a much lesser one. And probably felt under a cloud.**

Perhaps that was why his 9-year-old son Peter, whose dog Bruce had been bought for the child as a puppy, gave the terrier to Loxley to keep him company during his new command.

**The transfer to *Formidable* also denied Loxley a greater role in the prosecution of the war at sea, for *Inflexible* was to gain three battle honours, Falklands Islands, 8 December 1914; Dardanelles, 1915; and Jutland, 31 May 1916.

3

The Quickening Tide

There is a tide in the affairs of men
Which, taken at the flood, leads on to fortune;
Omitted, all the voyage of their life
Is bound in shallows and in miseries.
(William Shakespeare, *Julius Caesar*, Act 4)

The Fifth Battle Squadron was part of the Channel Fleet, tasked with patrolling the Straits of Dover and preventing the German navy from interfering with the dispositions and transport required by the British army. Initially commanded by Vice-Admiral Sir Cecil Burney (whose son-in-law was serving as commander on HMS *Formidable*) it comprised mainly pre-dreadnought battleships and light cruisers forming the Fifth, Sixth, Seventh and Eighth Battle Squadrons (the latter two having been part of the 'Third Fleet' until the outbreak of war and laid up in port). Apart from *Formidable*, the other ships in the Fifth Battle Squadron were *Prince of Wales* (Flag), *Bulwark*, *London*, *Venerable*, *Queen*, *Irresistible*, *Implacable*, and the light cruisers *Topaze* and *Diamond*. Later HMS *Lord Nelson*, flagship of the Channel Fleet, and HMS *Agamemnon* were included in the squadron. Each large ship was crewed by around 750 men.

The men of *Formidable*, and her sisters, were full time

professional Royal Navy, Royal Naval Reserve (yachtsmen, coastguards, merchant seamen, trawler men and others interested in the sea who signed up for so many weeks' service per year) and volunteers. Of the latter two categories, many of the RNR men had been serving on manoeuvres at the test mobilisation of July 1914 and were thus in place from the beginning of the conflict, and the volunteers were those who had joined up in the first flush of patriotic fervour in the early months of the war.

The navy had been chronically short of men before the war, one of the reasons behind Fisher's 'nucleus crew' concept, and this lack can be seen in the make-up of the full time crew of the *Formidable*. There were around seventy-five 'boys', lads generally aged 14 to 16 fresh from training ships, often from destitute homes, who were effectively 'apprentice seamen'. There was also a cadre of some fourteen midshipmen, aged 16 or so, trainee officers who had previously undertaken two years' education at HMS *Britannia*, the navy's cadet school.

Conscription had not yet been introduced and would not come into force until 1916 with the passage of Asquith's Military Service Act, which provided for the mandatory call up of all single men aged 18–41 who were not widowed with children or ministers of religion. Coming into effect on March 2nd, the act was amended in June to provide for the call up of married men too.

Prior to the Military Services Act, recruitment to the forces had relied on patriotism, moral pressure (the 'white feather' movement for example) and the desire to gain some excitement before – as was widely expected – it was 'all over by Christmas'. There was also a possible economic reason for enlistment: unemployment rose sharply after the declaration of war (July unemployment rate 2.8%; August 7%) as industry lost access to raw materials or cut back production in expectation of reduced demand. It was under such influences as these that the volunteers aboard *Formidable* had joined up.

While not able to stand in line of battle against dread-noughts, the squadron could nonetheless fight smaller ships or its own kind. Initially based at Portland, in November they returned to Sheerness amid fears of a German invasion of the east coast, where they would be called upon to disrupt any invading armada. It is strange that, in the years leading up to the war, Britain and its politicians were seized by the thought of invasion and much argument was expended concerning the need to retain soldiers at home, rather than sending them to France, to deal with this threat, and also concerning where the navy should be stationed to meet it. Books such as Erskine Childers' *The Riddle of the Sands* (1903) and *The Invasion of 1910* by William Le Queux, serialised by the *Daily Mail* in 1906, had stoked such fears, as had Guy du Maurier's play *An Englishman's Home* of 1909, which ran uninterrupted for 18 months. In 1908 the Committee of Imperial Defence had appointed an invasion inquiry, before which former Prime Minister A.J. Balfour, among others, testified. The conclusion was that a successful invasion could not be mounted, but the public were not aware of this and the 'idea of invasion became almost a psychosis'.[1] In reality the Germans had no such plans – it was a complete red herring.

Back at Sheerness the Fifth Battle Squadron remained at anchor, their routine largely peaceful, but on November 21st it was interrupted by a powerful internal explosion aboard *Formidable*'s half-sister HMS *Bulwark*, which blew up while moored at number 17 buoy in Kethole Reach, four miles west of Sheerness in the estuary of the river Medway. All of her officers were lost, and out of her complement of 750, only fourteen sailors survived; two of these men subsequently died of their injuries in hospital, and almost all of the remaining survivors were seriously injured. The only men to survive the explosion comparatively unscathed were those who had been in number 1 mess deck amidships, who were blown out of an open hatch. Witnesses on the battleship *Implacable*, the next ship in line at the mooring, reported that 'a huge pillar of black cloud belched upwards ... From the depths of this writhing column flames appeared running down to sea level.' The curtains to the *Bulwark*'s captain's cabin were later found to have been blown onto *Formidable*'s deck. The most detailed descriptions of the disaster came from witnesses on board battleships *Prince of Wales* and *Agamemnon*, who stated that smoke issued from the stern of the ship prior to the explosion and that the first explosion appeared to take place in an after magazine.

A naval court of inquiry into the causes of the explosion, held on November 28th, established that it had been the practice to store ammunition for the *Bulwark*'s 6-inch guns in cross-passageways connecting her total of eleven magazines. It suggested that, contrary to regulations, more than two hundred 6-inch shells had been placed close together, most touching each other, and some touching the walls of the magazine, on the morning of the explosion. The most likely cause of the disaster appears to have been overheating of cordite charges stored alongside a boiler room bulkhead, and this was the explanation accepted by the court of inquiry. One of the Fifth Battle Squadron family was gone; and through carelessness or want of consideration.

Bulwark was the second Royal Navy battleship to be sunk since the start of the war. In terms of *materiel* the loss was less than catastrophic. But the loss of so many men, even if not all were fully trained, was a disaster.

So too was the sinking of the first battleship to be lost, the modern dreadnought HMS *Audacious*. On August 27th *Audacious* hit a mine while exercising off the coast of Ireland. The ship rapidly began to list, and the passing liner *Olympic*, sister to the ill-fated *Titanic*, hove-to to assist. The battleship's crew took to the boats and were picked up by the liner which then tried to take the *Audacious* in tow, a manoeuvre that proved impossible. Vice-Admiral Sir Lewis Bayly, then commanding the First Battle Squadron, arrived on the scene in the boarding vessel *Cambria* and took over the rescue operation but, with darkness approaching, Bayly and the remaining men on *Audacious* were taken off at 19:15. Shortly afterwards, *Audacious* rolled, turned turtle, blew up and sank. Fortunately there were no losses among the crew. An interesting aspect to this sinking is that the Admiralty covered it up for the whole of the war, binding the liner's passengers to silence, in order to prevent the Germans knowing that the margin of superiority held by the Grand Fleet had been eroded.

Now came a change of command for the Channel Fleet. On December 17th the aforementioned Vice-Admiral Bayly assumed command. When he took charge the Sixth Battle Squadron were conducting gunnery exercises off Portland, and his first thought was to deploy the Fifth against the German coast in retaliation for the recent German bombardment of Scarborough. However this was turned down by the Admiralty, as insufficient anti-mine and anti-submarine resources could be spared. Told that he might be so deployed at a later date, Bayly instead requested that the Fifth Battle Squadron be sent to Portland in succession to the Sixth for sea exercises and battle practice. The Admiralty agreed to this request and gave him permission for the squadron to sail, with the usual caution to arrange his passage with due regard to the possibility of submarine attack *en route*. The practice of the day for squadrons moving through the Straits was to time their sailing so as to pass the narrows in the night or, if a daylight passage was unavoidable, not to move without destroyer protection. And so, on December 30th, the squadron departed their moorings. Weather conditions were poor and a strong wind and tide were running. In fact the weather had been awful all December, with only six rain-free days; the wettest December for 40 years. Towards the end of the month the country was continuously battered by strong south-westerly gales which damaged buildings and caused fatalities in London, Kent, Essex and the south west. It was a very nasty time to be at sea.

Bayly was a strong character and a man of fixed opinions. Like many of his contemporaries, he had a 'slight contempt for the submarine ... he just would not believe in [them]'.[2] Given the weather, and the fact that no submarine activity had been reported in the area, he disdainfully declined the destroyer escort sent by the Admiralty – whose role was anti-submarine defence – for the voyage. The Chief of Staff (Admiral Sturdee) sent him six destroyers anyway and they sailed with the battleships from Sheerness. As the squadron passed Folkestone during the afternoon the escort destroyers departed, as per Admiralty orders, leaving only the two light cruisers of the smaller ships. Bayly, in his flagship *Lord Nelson*, led his squadron in line-ahead formation steaming at a gentle 10 knots. *Topaze* and *Diamond* were stationed a mile astern of the last battleship, *Formidable*. Bayly did not order the fleet to zig-zag, the standard defence against U-boat attack, reckoning the loss of time, increased fuel consumption and difficulty of station keeping in the poor weather outweighed any risk, although the squadron was unguarded. It had no flotilla or cruiser squadron, excepting the two attached light cruisers, and it was therefore peculiarly exposed to torpedo attack.

By first light on the 31st the Fifth Battle Squadron was approximately thirteen miles south of Portland Bill and with a severe gale expected the ships battened down for heavy seas. The admiral gained first-hand experience of the growing severity of the weather when his flagship, HMS *Lord Nelson* – the last pre-dreadnought ever to be commissioned and weighing in at 17,820 tons – had to pull out of the line of the

36

fleet in the early hours of the morning and steer due north to secure hatches on the forecastle which had been blown loose by the strength of the wind, re-joining the other ships at 0800 hours.

Bayly exercised his ships, steaming down towards Start Point and then turning onto a reciprocal course back towards St Alban's Head. The exercises, which were conducted within twenty-five miles of the Bill, lasted the greater part of the day. At their conclusion so free did the Channel appear to be from submarines, and so little did he think of the threat they posed, that the admiral decided to remain at sea despite the bad and worsening weather, and steamed south of the Isle of Wight towards Start Point, intending to continue the exercises the next day.

It is typical of the man that he did not order his ships into Portland harbour to avoid the severe weather or to allow for the celebration of the New Year. Hard and unemotional, Bayly kept them at it. In line ahead. At ten knots. In bright moonlight. Without zig-zagging. Without an escort.

4

U-24

War is nothing but a duel on a large scale.
(Carl von Clausewitz, *War, Politics and Power*)

U-24 was a German *Unterseeboot* – literally 'underwater boat'. Built in 1912 as a patrol submarine, she was armed with four torpedo tubes firing 20-inch torpedoes (which could carry a 362-lb charge of TNT for up to 3,500 yards) and a 3.4-inch gun. One of the first class of German submarines to be powered by a diesel engine, her gun was of larger calibre than her predecessors to allow her to attack merchant ships on the surface and thus save on expenditure of torpedoes. Capable of 17 knots on the surface and 9–10 when dived, she carried a complement of thirty-five men under 32-year-old Kapitänleutnant Rudolph Schneider, known as Rudi, a Kapitänleutnant since 1912.

Submarines were relatively new, and a much reviled and distrusted class of ship. Many sailors thought them a dishonourable and underhand weapon, suitable only for weaker nations and then only for coastal defence. Former First Sea Lord Sir Arthur Wilson VC, as an example, thought that their crews should be hanged as pirates if captured and while in office he did much to retard the development of the weapon for the British navy. In 1911 the Inspecting Captain of

Submarines (the man in charge of the navy's submarine development and training) was Captain Sydney Hall. He was a man of firm opinions and at odds with Wilson on tactical matters, particularly the pace of building new submarines and the type of boat which should be built. When it appeared to Wilson that Hall was getting too close to the engineering companies building the navy's submarines, Wilson took the opportunity to fire him from his post and assigned him to an old and useless third class cruiser, HMS *Diana*, based off Crete.

It was the tradition that the departing officer had the right to nominate his own successor. Hall nominated Captain Frank Brandt, a navy 'brain' and at the time in charge of the Eighth Submarine Flotilla. Wilson overruled this and appointed the more congenial Roger Keyes instead. But Wilson's desire to impose his own will on submarine development did not stop there. Brandt, a submarine specialist, never got another decent posting. He was assigned first to an old (1894) and wretched second class protected cruiser, HMS *Eclipse*, and in July 1914 to HMS *Monmouth*, then in the Third Fleet. He took her to die a fiery death at the Battle of Coronel on 1 November 1914.

The general attitude of most senior officers of the period could be summed up by the comments of Brandt's admiral at Coronel, Rear Admiral Sir Christopher Cradock, to his friend Roger Keyes, the new Inspecting Captain of Submarines: 'It would be far more satisfactory to these "playthings" to know whether they were observed or made hits or misses ... I am sure you will know what to do'.[1] 'Playthings' was the common view.

But one man who clearly saw that submarines had revolutionised naval warfare was Jackie Fisher, quondam First Sea Lord, and the man who created the *Dreadnought*. Fisher had driven the introduction of submarines and when out of office continually badgered First Lord Winston Churchill to increase the numbers being built. More than anyone, Fisher recognised that the advent of the torpedo-armed submarine meant the narrow waters of the North Sea and English Channel became a very high-risk environment for large and expensive capital ships. Rather than risk battleships in such a situation it was better, he argued, to police those waters through 'flotilla defence', using large numbers of torpedo boats (surface vessels carrying on deck torpedoes), submarines and torpedo boat destroyers (more usually abbreviated to 'destroyers') to render the waters uninhabitable for enemy battleships, potential invasion fleets and the like. Fisher's was something of a lone voice in the wilderness for much of the early part of the twentieth century, although he was not without support. Rear Admiral Frederick E.E. Brock, commanding the Portsmouth Division, Home Fleet, wrote to the then First Lord, McKenna, in March 1910 referring to the recently published Naval Estimates for 1910/11 and insisting, '... how much I think that the additional men and destroyers provided for are required in addition to the battleships'.[2]

Nonetheless, at the outbreak of war Britain had nowhere near enough such craft to pursue such a policy, and settled for patrols by destroyers, old cruisers and pre-dreadnought battleships such as *Formidable*.

That this was a strategy fraught with danger took hardly any time to prove. On 5 September 1914 the light cruiser HMS *Pathfinder* was patrolling off St Abbs Head in the North Sea when she was torpedoed by the German submarine U-21. The explosion touched off the forward magazine and the ship blew up and sank, with the loss of 250 men. The Admiralty, unwilling to admit that it was a submarine victory, announced that the vessel had hit a mine and, when that was exposed as a fallacy, stated that the submarine concerned had been cornered by cruisers and shelled to death. Neither point was true. *Pathfinder* gained the dubious distinction of being the first British warship to be sunk by a locomotive torpedo.

Then, on 22 September, three old armoured cruisers were patrolling off the Dutch coast. They had been, as Battenberg (First Sea Lord at the time) put it, 'peddling up and down' here since the outbreak of war to keep an eye on possible German light craft activity. They were elderly, vulnerable and predictable. Officially called 'Force C', they were known in the navy as 'the live bait squadron'. At 0630 the *Aboukir* was hit by a torpedo and sank. The *Hogue* was trying to rescue survivors when she too was hit and sank in 10 minutes. The *Cressy*, which by now should have been running for her life, unbelievably hove-to and at 0717 capsized having been hit by two torpedoes. All three ships had been sunk by one submarine, U-9, commanded by Kapitänleutnant Otto Weddigen. Sixty-two officers and 1,397 men (mostly middle-aged reservists and cadets straight out of the Dartmouth naval college) went down with their ships – ships that were of little or no value; but the men were.

Three weeks later on 15 October, U-9, once again on patrol in the North Sea, torpedoed the ancient cruiser HMS *Hawke*, resulting in the death of 524 men. Then on October 31st HMS *Hermes*, a seaplane carrier, was torpedoed while cruising in the Straits of Dover by U-27 and sank with the loss of twenty-two crew. Finally, HMS *Niger*, a converted minesweeper, was sunk by U-12 off the Downs (the coast of Deal in Kent) on 11 November, fortunately with only one crew member lost.

It should thus have been fairly plain to any naval officer operating around the British coast that there was a clear and present danger of submarine attack.

Attempts had been made to supplement the surface force protection with minefields at the entrance to the Dover Straits (laid after U-18 had entered the Straits on 27 September and fired a torpedo, which missed, at HMS *Attentive*) but British mines were both in short supply and of inferior quality. A twenty-five-kilometre barrage of sunken steel nets and mesh was also planned (the Dover barrage) which it was

hoped would ensnare submerged submarines. But this did
not come into use until February 1915 (and even then German commanders found it relatively easy to circumvent).
Likewise naval architects had begun fitting ships with 'torpedo bulges', caissons of steel protecting the hull of the
vessel, and hanging torpedo nets around ships when at
anchor. *Formidable* and her sisters, however, had not been
retrofitted with bulges and were vulnerable to underwater
attack in exactly the same way as the unfortunate old cruisers
which had fallen victim to Kapitänleutnant Weddigen.

Meanwhile, *Formidable* and the Fifth Battle Squadron were
trolling around in the dark. All ships had been darkened at
nightfall and at 1900 the fleet turned through sixteen points
in accordance with an Admiralty Fleet Order requiring an
alteration of course soon after dark in areas where a submarine attack was possible – a manoeuvre which fits uneasily
with Bayly's later claim that he had assumed from previous
Admiralty orders that no submarines would be encountered.

Kapitänleutnant Schneider was well aware of the successes
of his fellow countryman and was determined to emulate
them. He had slipped into the Channel from his base on the
Belgian coast, avoiding the Dover defences easily. On 31
December, lurking off Portland harbour and waiting for prey,
he had spotted the Sixth Battle Squadron, which had been on
exercises, steaming away from Portland. Later he sighted
three large warships steaming down the channel and decided
to shadow them. There was a very heavy sea running but
visibility was good throughout the day and into the evening
and he found trailing them easy, particularly as they were
cruising at modest speed and were not zig-zagging. Just after
midnight on January 1st 1915, aided by a full moon, Kapitänleutnant Schneider was able to identify the three vessels
he had been shadowing by their silhouettes as battleships.

Manoeuvring U-24 towards them undetected, he selected his target and fired one torpedo at HMS *Queen*, which missed.

At 0200 the fleet was again turned through sixteen points – in succession, which meant that they all executed their turn in the same place. A little later Schneider saw five large warships which appeared to have become detached from the other three. They were *Formidable* and some of her sisters in the Fifth Battle Squadron. *Formidable* was steaming at ten knots at the rear of the line, off Portland Bill, just twenty nautical miles from Start Point. In truth she was probably glad to be steaming slowly; the months of Channel patrol had worn her condensers and her engines were giving the engineering team some problems.

Stately, vast, a city of iron and steel and men, buffeting her way through wind, rain and a heavy, rising sea, *Formidable* swam into the sights of Schneider's periscope. Calmly and with a sense of rising anticipation he gave the fateful order: '*Los.*'

5

On Board HMS Formidable

Blood is the god of war's rich livery.
(Christopher Marlowe, *Tamburlaine the Great*)

Formidable's crew had welcomed in the New Year by rat-
tling tin cans down the ladders. At midnight sixteen bells had
been struck – eight bells for the old year and eight bells for
the new – to welcome the first morning of 1915. It was not to
be an auspicious one.

Schneider's torpedo struck her at 0220. It hit amidships on
the starboard side under the forward funnel, exploding
directly beneath the bridge in number 2 boiler room. It made a
hole the 'size of the proverbial bus'[1] in her side and also put
out of action the dynamo room, thereby robbing her of light-
ing and power for the wireless and other electrical apparatus.

Captain Loxley was on the bridge when the explosion
occurred. His immediate thought, perhaps with the example
of *Audacious* on his mind, was that they had hit a mine. It
being the middle watch, and the ship stood down from action
stations, the majority of the men were below decks sleeping,
some 500 in all. More were in the engine and boiler rooms.

Loxley swiftly followed standard procedure, ordering all
watertight doors to be shut and sounding 'collision stations'
by bugle. He turned his ship, which had already taken a

44

severe list, into the wind and the rising sea. Water was pouring into the battleship and started to flood the engine room. Fire was drawn from the boilers to reduce the risk of an internal explosion and as a result the steam pressure rapidly fell to zero; all electrical power had already been lost. To try to counteract the list, Loxley ordered the gunners to train the two big turrets on the beam but the hydraulic pressure had gone and the big guns could not be moved. Stumbling up from the dark bowels of the ship, sleep drugged, undressed or in pyjamas and unwary, men began to arrive on deck and at their collision posts.

By now, however, the ship had assumed a twenty-degree list to starboard and was drifting without power or lights in weather conditions that had already been bad and were now rapidly deteriorating. Slowly, the old girl was dying. But amidst the chaos and darkness the crew remained calm. Training and discipline among the experienced men took hold and there was no panic. Men stopped to salute their officers. Someone played ragtime on the piano, until that instrument was committed to the seas as a potential raft. 'A piano's better than now't,' someone said.[2] One sailor ran to the quarterdeck and found everyone smoking. 'I borrowed a cigarette from an officer and a light from a mate and even then went below to get more fags.'[3]

It was clear to Loxley that *Formidable* was very unlikely to survive and he ordered the ship's boats to be launched. *Formidable* carried a full complement of auxiliary boats. There were two 56-foot steam pinnaces, one 36-foot pinnace, one 36-foot sailing pinnace, one 40-foot sailing launch, two 34-foot cutters and one 30-foot cutter, three 27-foot whalers, one 28-foot gig, one 16-foot dinghy, and a 13-foot balsa raft. However, the angle of the ship's list to starboard meant that only boats on that side could be used. None of the steam pinnaces was launched. A survivor commented, 'We were very lucky to get any boats launched at all.'[4]

Where were *Formidable*'s sister ships? HMS *London* had noticed *Formidable* leave the line and signalled the flagship but gave no explanation. With the loss of electrical power *Formidable* was unable to use her wireless equipment. The light cruisers *Topaze* (Captain Law) and *Diamond* (Commander Dundas) could see what was happening and closed towards the stricken ship but the height of the seas made it difficult for them to provide assistance. On board HMS *Diamond* there was consternation. Corporal F.E. Little remembered that it was a clear moonlit night. Then he heard people shouting, 'Here, the *Formidable*'s going out of line! She's heeling. She's been hit!' All the crew were called from below decks 'and we received instructions from the Flagship to assist'.[5] But the cruisers, weighing in at only 3,000 tons, 360 feet long and, in the case of *Topaze*, decommissioned to the Third Fleet for scrapping in 1913 until war broke out, were being tossed around the waves like toys.

Topaze had signalled the flagship that *Formidable* had been torpedoed by a submarine. Bayly immediately followed Admiralty standing orders when encountering submarines in such circumstances and ordered his ships to change course and run towards Portland at full speed. *Topaze* and *Diamond* were ordered to remain with *Formidable* and continue the rescue attempt. Torpedo boats and small craft were instructed to sail from Devonport and Portland, but in the appalling weather it was impossible for them to make any progress from harbour and they were forced to return

Topaze closed *Formidable* to render assistance, circling round the battleship. Boats and swimmers could be seen in the water and the crew tried to get hold of them, but the heavy sea made the work difficult and hazardous. Still, *Topaze* had succeeded in rescuing forty-three men out of a barge and the sea when Captain Loxley ordered her to go off to close a brilliantly lighted liner that was passing and direct her to stand by. A liner would have been an ideal rescue ship.

Diamond immediately took her place, but though *Topaze* passed the order to the liner and it was acknowledged, the liner continued her course. Rockets and lights from the *Formidable* made no impression on her either and *Topaze* returned to the sinking ship. The liner's captain, had he but known it, had just condemned many men to a watery grave.

Meanwhile, aboard U-24 Schneider wanted to make sure of his kill and had loitered in the area unmolested. Seeing that his victim had not yet foundered, he worked round to her port side and fired another torpedo. This one hit below the after funnel and exploded in number 1 boiler room. It was *Formidable*'s death warrant, but perversely had the effect of bringing her back onto an even keel. She started to settle, lying lower in the huge seas which now broke over her main decks and rushed into her hull, both through the external wounds and through topside hatches and doors, trapping many men in the engine room and boiler spaces.

Despite the return to an even keel, it was proving difficult to launch the heavier ship's boats as there was no steam power to the cranes and winches. In any event some were already damaged beyond use by the explosions and the movements brought about by the initial angle of list, and there was no steam up in the steam-powered pinnaces. All available portable material which would float was thrown overboard to help keep men buoyant in the water. The hooter was sounded continuously and the signalmen fired off flares.

Realising that the submarine was still in the area, Loxley selflessly signalled the cruisers to stand off to avoid them becoming victims themselves, the example of 'Force C' perhaps uppermost in his mind, and to go after another steamer which had appeared on the horizon. But in the worsening weather that too disappeared from sight.

With the ship's boats largely useless, desperate measures had been taken to acquire anything that would float. Chairs and tables were thrown overboard and the ship's carpenters had even begun to wrench up the deck planking. Loxley knew that *Formidable* was finished. Standing on the bridge with his commander and signalmen he gave the order to abandon ship. His dog Bruce stood with him.

As the old lady began to sink into the rough seas it became every man for himself. Many jumped into the enormous waves and were immediately drowned or dashed against the ship's side. Now she dipped down by the bow, like a maiden's curtsey, and then wearily turned over onto her starboard side. Those who had clung to the illusion of safety on deck had clambered up to the port side guardrails and as she turned over they slid down the ship's hull, only to bash against the bilge keel and then fall battered and helpless into the sea. Others fell rather than slid, so steep was the incline, across the deck, smashing into the turrets and other impedimenta and being horribly injured. Just after 0430 she died and began the descent to the bottom of the English Channel and her final resting place, thirty miles south of Lyme Regis.

There were many acts of heroism reported during those hours between the first torpedo and the final sinking. There were nearly 100 boys and midshipmen in the ship's company, some as young as 14, drafted at the outbreak of war to beef up the nucleus crew. The ship's company felt quite protective towards them and many sailors gave them their outer clothes to keep them warm. 'It was middies first all the way,' said one survivor.[6] Not many survived despite this rough chivalry.

The ship's chaplain was Reverend George Brooke-Robinson who had been a navy chaplain for sixteen years. In 1900 he was part of the team on HMS *Theseus* who surveyed the total eclipse of the sun (on 28th May) from Santa Pola, which was later the subject of a lecture at the Royal Institution. 1908 found him serving on HMS *Sapphire*, sister ship to his potential rescuers *Diamond* and *Topaze*. In 1910/11 he was chaplain to Admiral Richard Poore when, as CinC, Poore took a flying squadron to Australia. While in Hobart, Tasmania, in February 1911, Robinson had preached at that city's Holy Trinity Church. He was married (to Alice Irene) and, with a morbid circularity, had once been curate of Burton Bradstock parish church and a keen and prominent swimmer at the West Bay Swimming Club. Now his ship was sinking in close proximity to them both.

Brooke-Robinson, seeking to provide comfort for the men, went back down into the ship to get more cigarettes. When he re-emerged on the quarterdeck the few boats to be launched had pulled away. He reassured those with him, "'Stay on the ship. Wait for the escort to come." He was confident that his friend – the first lieutenant of one of the escort cruisers – would come for them when he discovered that he (the chaplain) was missing. The chaplain had officiated at that officer's wedding; they were brothers-in-law.'[7] His altruism did not save him, however, for he was one of the men to die sliding down the ship's side.

A party of men led by Lieutenant George H.V. Hawthorn RMLI, armed with a small flashlight, had bravely gone into the darkness of the dying battleship in search of anything that could act as a life preserver. Hawthorn continued to collect chairs and other floatable material from the marines' mess deck even when it was apparent that the ship might capsize at any moment. Perhaps unsurprisingly, he did not survive.

Twenty-two-year-old Sub Lieutenant Herbert F.C. Shinnie, a proud Scot and a reserve officer called to the colours, superintended the lowering of the quarterdeck boats, and when Loxley ordered abandon ship he went to each of the men near him to ensure that they had something about them which would float. He himself had nothing, and went down with the ship.

The stokers also performed magnificently. Sticking to their posts they drew all the fires in the twenty water-tube boilers, which would otherwise have caused a massive engine room explosion as the *Formidable* sank. As a result some were trapped below and were dragged down with her. In fact 85% of her stokers were lost, compared to 66% of general seamen. The gunners had also been ordered to stand to their posts in case of further surface attack. They too suffered as a result.

The medical department of the *Formidable* suffered disproportionately in the aftermath of the sinking. She had on board three surgeons and ten sick bay attendants. Only two of the latter survived. Fleet Surgeon (roughly equivalent to a commander in rank) Godfrey Taylor, Surgeon William Mearns and Surgeon Septimus Hibbert (RNVR – the volunteer reserve) all lost their lives. Were they looking after the sick and injured right up to the end? Or, as medical men, perhaps they were not inured to the cold and mountainous seas in the way a sea-officer might be.

Stanley Reed, a 16-year-old Royal Marine bugler, was another who demonstrated selfless courage. A colleague suggested to him that he should use his drum to keep afloat. But Reed had given it to a sailor who had no floatation collar. Reed stayed on board to the last and sounded the final bugle call, 'every man for himself'. He was later seen in the water holding a piece of wood but did not survive the heavy sea and cold.

As already noted above, it was barely possible to launch the ship's boats. After a superhuman effort the crew managed to get four of the craft away. The first capsized immediately, tossing her twelve-man crew into the terrifying sea that whisked ten of them away to their deaths; two of the men were miraculously swept back onto the ship, alive albeit severely crushed. The second boat to be launched made the tricky journey right around the battleship to her port side where men were lining the guardrails. 'Fifty men only! Now then, you fellows play the game,' shouted the bo'sun.[8] The men made no violent rushes to the rails. Discipline held.

Despite the sheer drop of twenty-five feet that lay between them and the fragile launch they swarmed down the side using ropes, blankets and any article to hand, while others risked the jump. Among the men who jumped was Stoker First Class Harold Smithurst, a reservist who in civilian life played the piano at a picture palace in Hammersmith. He it was who had played some ragtime tunes before the ship's piano had been heaved overboard. As the cutter came around the port side of the ship he dropped into her, falling a distance of over twenty feet and injuring himself badly on landing. 'No more,' yelled the bo'sun. 'Good luck boys!'[9] The boat sailed off into the dark, leaving the remainder to take their chance. Smithurst grabbed an oar and rowed for all he was worth, fighting back the pain.

But it was Noel Loxley who made the greatest impression. Loxley stayed on the forebridge, directing operations, the whole time. His cool and calm demeanour made a great impression. 'Cool as a cucumber,' commented one survivor, 'just as if the ship was riding in harbour with the anchors down. The last words I heard him say were "Steady men; it's all right. No panic, men. Keep cool. Be British. There's life in the old ship yet." You cannot speak his praises too much and the same is true of Lieutenant Simonds who worked magnificently in getting out the boats.'[10] Another survivor heard Loxley complement Simonds. 'The last I saw of Captain Loxley he was on the bridge calmly smoking a cigarette. Lieutenant Simonds was supervising the launching of the boats and as he got the last away I heard the Captain say, "You have done well, Simonds".'*[11]

Loxley, his second in command Commander Ballard, and a signalman stuck to the task of sending off red and green distress flares and signals to the very end. When the ship finally gave a mighty lurch Loxley shouted to the remaining

---

*Simonds was plucked from the sea by HMS *Diamond*, and survived.

crew, 'Lads, this is the last, all hands for themselves, and may God bless you and guide you to safety.'[12] He then walked to the forebridge, lit a cigarette and, with his terrier Bruce loyally at his side, waited for the end, in true naval tradition. He, Commander Ballard, and Bruce went down with the ship.

The old girl went down by the bow. For a minute or two she hung with her screws out of the water and her rudder swinging from side to side, as though she was stuck on the bottom. Then she disappeared from sight. Even as the *Formidable* slipped beneath the clamouring sea, a survivor in one of the boats noted that 'just as she was taking her final plunge there were flashes from the bridge – the last signal sent out by our captain'.[13]

6

The Struggle

When we sailed into a raging storm
Like I've never ever seen before;
And all of the crew they were brave men,
But the captain, he was braver,
He said "Never mind the ship, me boys,
There's none of us here can save her."
Let her go down,
Swim for your lives.

(Peter Knight)

The raging sea was filled with debris and men and boys, some dead, many injured, some struggling to stay alive. It had only been possible to launch five boats and one had been immediately destroyed. The light cruiser *Topaze* had managed to rescue forty-three men from a boat and the water, and *Diamond* thirty-seven men from the sea, of whom ten were officers and midshipmen. The high proportion of officers saved was due in part to the fact that they eschewed the standard issue Royal Navy swimming collar, which was wholly unfitted to its purpose, and instead were wearing Gieves waistcoats – an early type of life jacket and purchased privately from Gieves the naval outfitters.

Many sailors, unable to find a place in a boat, had taken to the unforgiving waters of the Channel. And there most would die from exposure. The water temperature was below 7 degrees centigrade. At this temperature hypothermia sets in quickly as core body temperature drops. Any body temperature below 35 degrees will produce a hypothermic reaction. Difficulty in speaking, sluggish thinking, and amnesia start to appear. Sufferers lose the ability to use their hands and legs. Cellular metabolic processes shut down. Below thirty degrees centigrade the exposed skin turns blue and puffy, muscle coordination becomes very poor and the victim exhibits incoherent behaviour, frequently ending in stupor. Below twenty-four degrees a severe reaction occurs. Pulse and respiration rates decrease significantly. Major organs fail. Clinical death follows, although here drowning frequently and perhaps mercifully often supervened.

However, there were survivors, although there must have been times in the long ordeal to follow when they would probably have preferred a quick and easy death. For some, courage, determination and unquenchable stamina carried them through. For others, survival depended on the actions of crewmates. And for a few, the hand of destiny seemed to take a part.

Able Seaman Tom Walker, who had been recently promoted, had just received his back pay and a new gold sovereign which he was keeping in his kit locker for his mother. When the alarm was sounded he was on deck and joined the men waiting to get into the boats. Remembering his sovereign, he dashed back below decks in the dark and returned to the quarterdeck in a panic to find it deserted, apart from Chaplain Brooke-Robinson who calmed him down. As the ship began to turn over for the final time Walker, the chaplain and the remaining men went over the port guardrail and slid down the side, sitting on the ship's bottom until she started to go under. As he plunged into the sea Walker grabbed a passing wooden boom but was struck a heavy blow on the leg by the ship's propeller and thought he was badly hurt. For hours he and others nearby tried to keep awake and afloat, singing hymns and praying, until he heard his ship's name being called. The light cruiser HMS *Diamond* had found him, a line was thrown, and suddenly he was being rubbed dry on a mess table, and safe.

Twenty-six-year-old Assistant Paymaster Sidney Saxton had injured himself sliding down the keel. Briefly hanging onto the propellers before she went down he sighted a ship in the distance and by instinct he made to swim for her. When he eventually reached her, no doubt helped by his Gieves life-jacket, he found himself so weak that he could not summon the strength to haul himself up the side. He was about to give up when a huge wave caught him and hurled him onto the deck. Saxton was saved and boarded *Diamond* by the most unlikely of methods.

Able Seaman Jack Fisher had joined the navy in 1911 as a Boy Second Class, aged 17, having worked previously as a shorthand typist. Born in the flatlands of Diss, Norfolk, he was assigned to *Formidable* in 1913 and rated AB in the November. He must have taken some stick in the mess, given that he shared his name with one of the navy's most iconic figures who, in January 1915, was First Sea Lord. However, the ribbing, Diss, and its placid Mere must all have seemed preferable as he found himself fighting for his life in the heaving seas. A dim shape loomed out of the murk and he struck out towards it, grabbed hold of a dangling line and was hauled aboard *Topaze*. He was one of the lucky ones.

Seaman Gunner William Hughes was on watch with his gun crew when the first torpedo struck. He remembered the ship taking a gradual list and the smell of spent explosives from the weapon in the air. He found a place in the 34-foot cutter and pulled away from the ship, personally picking up six or seven men who were swimming in the water. From their position near the bows of *Formidable*, they saw the second torpedo strike home and the old battleship begin to settle. 'There was no panic [on board],' he stated, 'absolutely nothing; it was as if nothing had happened at all ... they were singing *Tipperary* and we sang it in our boat too. Some men were smoking; one man in our boat asked a Lieutenant for a fag and he got it off him.'[1]

A 'gigantic explosion' awoke Leading Stoker William Parr at around 0200, he recalled. He and his mates rushed up on deck half-dressed but there was no panic. It was impossible to launch the steam pinnaces and he helped to get the sailing one away instead, securing a place in it. According to his account they stood off for an hour in the hope of saving more of their comrades but in vain.[2]

Petty Officer Bing had been in the after turret and was so sure that the sound of the torpedo hitting was gunfire that he started to load his gun. Then he heard 'collision stations' sounded and hurried to assist in getting the boats out. Another gunner, Daniel Horrigan, was in a turret at 2.10 am when he heard a crash on the starboard side of the ship. As he was leaving his post he ran into Commander Ballard who told him to tell everyone he met to keep cool. Ballard was keen to get a big wooden gunnery target, which was stowed on deck, over the side to act as a flotation aid for men going into the water. Finding that there were not enough men to lift the heavy target, Horrigan ran off to the quarterdeck to get some help. 'As I was going over the other side of deck another explosion took place so near to where I stood that the shock of it flung me off the side of the ship into the water,' he later narrated. 'I floated for some time until I was picked up by the launch which all this time was well away from the ship but standing by to get more men.'[3] A cruiser came close to pick them up but then diverted away, and in the heavy seas they lost sight of it.

Marine Lance Corporal Ernest Hunt had, like so many others, been asleep before the explosion and rushed up on deck. When the second torpedo struck he was shot up into the air and landed in the water. As he surfaced from his involuntary ducking he saw the black shape of a boat and clutched at its side. However, all he managed to do was hurt his hand and he slipped back below the waves. 'I was saved by a piece of string [sic] attached to the rudder which I grasped and was pulled into the boat.'[4] Another marine, Private John George Mitchell, was knocked onto his back by the first explosion and disoriented by the lights going out. His first thought was to rouse the officers who were in their berths and then he went to the afterbridge to work the derricks and was able to help launch the cutter, after which he jumped into the sea and hauled himself aboard her.

Telegraphist George W. Wilson had just come off watch and turned into his hammock when he heard the explosion. He immediately assumed it was a torpedo and ran to assist in getting out the boats, marvelling at how quickly the watertight doors had been closed. He assisted in the launch of the sailing pinnace which was swung out but then crashed back into the bridge. The next attempt was more successful and she and the men in her dropped into the water, Wilson among them. The crew tried to work the pinnace around to the port side and were going alongside when the second explosion was seen. Huge spouts of water and quantities of coal were thrown up into the air and came down on the heads of the men in the little craft. They took on board as many as possible and then hauled off. 'The last I saw of the ship was the men smoking on the quarter deck and singing while the captain and commander were on the bridge, also the captain's dog,' he later recalled.[5]

Joseph Henry Taplin, Acting Leading Stoker, had been in his hammock when the first torpedo struck. In the dark and impeded by other hammocks and the ship's list he grabbed at some clothing and struggled up on deck, to find he had taken a pair of trousers and one sock. He was still on deck when the second torpedo struck and found himself flung into the sea.

Taplin was wearing his life-saving collar but he found it more trouble than it was worth and tried to remove it, eventually deflating it to get it off. Waves washed over him and he swam desperately and mechanically, his limbs growing weary, and beginning to feel dragged down. He felt sleepy, that he was lying on a soft bed (the classic symptoms of exposure) and then oblivion. He woke with a start to find that he was in a pinnace, with an oar thrust into his lifeless hands. The men in the boat told him he had been in the water for forty-five minutes. His hands and feet were swollen with the immersion, but he was alive. Little did he know that his ordeal was only just beginning.

Able Seaman Alfred Walter Booth had 'turned in', too tired after the day of evolutions to undress, two hours before he was wakened by the explosion of the torpedo. As the ship heeled over he fought against the list to gain the upper deck and his boat station. When the order to abandon ship was given he peered over the side into the crashing waves and did not like what he saw. Remembering too late that he had forgotten his lifejacket, he nonetheless kicked off his sea boots, murmured a prayer, took a deep breath and jumped. The cold hit him like a punch and he sank beneath the waves. Everything went black, His lungs felt as if they would burst. Lights flashed in his eyes; and then all went black. He came to in a pinnace, where strong arms had dragged him from the water, more dead than alive. He was safe, if safe included 30-foot waves and a howling gale battering the small craft. And, like Taplin's, his ordeal had only just started.

For Stoker First Class Reuben Smith, salvation came in a mysterious way. He had been ordered out of number 2 boiler room and was waiting on deck when the explosion of the second torpedo catapulted him over the side of the *Formidable*. He landed on the heads of the men in the boat below. It was a lucky escape, for the blast destroyed the boiler room he had just vacated.

Seventeen-year-old Boy First Class Eddison 'Eddie' Wheatley was also luckier than many. When he heard the captain order 'every man for himself' he jumped into the sea and swam to the cutter, hauling himself on board. 'I saw a lot of chaps who were weaker swimmers go down, including many of my mates,' he related later.[6]

It is difficult today for us to imagine the sheer terror that must have gripped *Formidable*'s crew as the old lady went down. It was dark, a gale was blowing, the waves were enormous and had crushed one of the few boats launched. Men were tipped into the sea as she went down, precipitated into the icy cold water, only to be caught up in a maelstrom of rigging and aerials. The suction caused by the great ship diving beneath the water tugged at and dragged some of them under as they tried frenziedly to escape. For the men already in the water, clinging to some means of support or relying solely on the inadequate flotation collars, there was small prospect of rescue. The waves heaved them about and prevented them from seeing either the ship's boats or the cruisers; and there was a real danger of being run down as the cruisers tried their best to locate survivors in the water. Heart rates were high with adrenalin and fear. Energy reserves, especially of the young, injured or unfit, were quickly depleted. As the cold and wet numbed their bodies and the first crippling symptoms of exposure took hold, it was all too easy to close their eyes and slip beneath the waves. One by one they died.

For the men in the pinnace and the cutter, unknowing of each other and seemingly alone on the tempestuous sea, the ordeal appeared to last for ever. Men died at the oars from exhaustion. Men slipped to the bottom of the boats to lie and die there. The hope of rescue began to slip away. Singing *Tipperary* could take a man only so far. Soon they were living in individual worlds of pain and terror, rowing or bailing mechanically, unthinkingly, automata in search of salvation.

And so the two boat-loads of sailors fought for their lives in the teeth of the storm. They did not see the cruisers, and the cruisers did not see them. They were on their own, left to wage their own private battle with the elemental forces ranged against them.

Topaze and *Diamond* remained in the area until first light. Believing there to be no prospect of rescuing any more survivors, both ships abandoned the search at 0814 and set a course towards Portland, some 20 miles away. It was a measure of the severity of the weather that it took more than ten hours to reach harbour and safety due to the now gale force winds and heavy seas. All survivors and witnesses stated that the weather conditions were appalling. At 0550 *Topaze*'s log describes the winds as southerly 'hurricane force and very heavy seas running'. Records show that the winds on the day peaked at force 11, at around 0900–1000. The description associated with such a reading on the Beaufort scale indicates a wind speed of 69 mph and a predicted wave height of 37 feet to 52 feet, equivalent to two and a half to three and a half times the height of a London Routemaster bus. *Topaze* had her 30-foot cutter, both top-gallant masts and her wireless aerials carried away by the winds. Nonetheless, Vice Admiral Bayly remained sanguine about there being more survivors. In a letter to the Admiralty on the day of the sinking he noted, 'It appears to me possible that some, in boats, may have been driven by the gale to leeward and that if they could withstand the sea and cold, may have landed near Lyme Regis or been picked up by fishing boats etc.'[7] In this, if nothing else, he was to be proved correct.

The sailing pinnace which had picked up Parr, Wilson, Taplin, Booth and Smith had taken 71 men on board. It was soon half-filled with water as the men desperately bailed – with boots, caps, even a blanket, anything that came to hand. Most were in only their undergarments, with only a couple of men fully dressed. One seaman sat over a hole in the boat for the entire duration of their ordeal to keep it plugged. The swell was enormous and the boat was regularly swamped. The rudder was swept away and the compasses had been lost. There was no food. Morale began to flag as energy loss, wet and cold dampened the initially enthusiastic singing and mutual support. It was a time for leaders to emerge and fortunately they did. Petty Officer Herbert Bing, a tall, strong, handsome man, bullied, cajoled and occasionally punched men to keep them focused on survival. Bing had only just made Petty Officer four weeks previously but he proved the wisdom of that promotion now. Leading Seaman Thomas Hanlon ('Micky') Carroll, coxswain of the boat, was another who emerged as a leader. A Kerry man who had joined the navy in 1895 at the age of 12, he continually inspired and hectored the men, keeping them at the tasks of bailing and rowing while attempting to steer the ship with a single oar. Many in the pinnace later credited him with their survival, in particular for his decision to run with the wind instead of putting the boat's head into it, as custom would have had it.

Dawn came with no sight of land. Wet, thirsty and tired, some just lay down and waited to die. Those who did die were thrown overboard with little ceremony, as the boat was full of water and would sink if the dead weight was not disposed of. The water was up to the men's waists as they rowed. Master-at-Arms Martin Cooper (the ship's 'policeman'), senior man in the pinnace, and Carroll restarted the singing, forcing the others to join in until all were hoarse from the effort. A liner was seen at 0500, and then up to eleven other craft, but the huge waves hid the pinnace. The whole day passed, night came, and still the winds were relentless.

Men continued to pass quietly into death, a sort of frozen sleep. One big seaman went mad, shouting orders, thrashing around and biting those nearest to him. Then he jumped

overboard and sank from sight. It began to rain, then hail –
but this was a godsend as the men were able to open their
mouths, faces turned upwards, and catch some precious
drops of fresh water on their tongues.

On land, blackout restrictions were in force and no lights
could be seen. But then Bing thought he saw a red light. He
didn't know what it was – it was probably the Lyme harbour
light. Joseph Taplin had a different, and if true more seren-
dipitous, explanation. He saw a sudden bright light three
miles off. It might have been the Assembly Rooms cinema.
The projector had broken down and the operator examining
it shone the lamp through the window for a second or two.
Whatever the explanation for the sightings, they represented
salvation for the men of the pinnace. There were only six
oars left now, but with aching arms and tired beyond
endurance they pulled towards the light. Bing gathered the
last of his strength to shout out, 'Pull boys, pull. You'll soon
be in.'

That night Miss Gwen Harding and her parents were
walking home along Lyme Regis's Marine Parade after dining
out with friends at the Standard Inn. She thought she saw the
faint outline of a boat struggling in the waves and surf. Her
mother concurred and together they raised the alarm. News
of the sighting reached Police Sergeant James Stockley, who
was on duty outside the Assembly Rooms with another officer, PC Rideout, just before 2300. Stockley and his colleague
ran to the seafront and near Cobb Gate saw a large open boat
heading through the surf and howling wind for the shore.
Sending his constable to get more help, Sergeant Stockley
went down to the littoral where he threw himself on a line
heaved out from the boat and pulled for all he was worth.

A sailor jumped from the pinnace into the water and
scrambled ashore to join him on the line. Another followed,
but weakened by exposure and exhaustion lost his grip and
was carried back into the sea. Stockley rushed into the heavy

surf, grabbed the sailor and with huge difficulty dragged him onto the beach. He then returned to the water to save two other exhausted men, despite being himself knocked over by the waves. One of those saved was Stoker James Connor, who later said that Stockley had saved his life: 'I know I owe my life to him as I could not hold the line any longer. He dragged me ashore just when I was being carried on the backwash of the surf.'[8] George Wilson managed to stagger onto the shore under his own steam but then collapsed to the ground exhausted. There was a momentary panic when someone on the beach noticed the boat's badge (*Formidable*'s crest, an eagle with spread wings) and confused it with the German Imperial emblem, saying that they should push the boat back into the sea. But Stockley told them not to be so stupid and more Lyme residents arrived at the Cobb to assist. Two local doctors, Cooper and Spurr, and a visiting physician, Patterson, all ran down to the beach to conduct triage and send the survivors to various public houses in the town for warmth and comfort. Bragg's grocery store threw open its doors and as the men staggered up the steps opposite Alcove Cottage to gain the safety of the land, Mrs Bragg made coffee and tea for the survivors. The one-time 'wreckers' of the Dorset coast were redeeming their old reputation.

Seventy-one men had started the horrific journey in the pinnace. During the dreadful 22-hour voyage fourteen had died and were buried in the seas that killed them. Fifty-one ragged, wet and shivering survivors staggered to the shore, leaving another six of their mates dead in the boat. Two who made the shoreline died on it of the final effects of exposure. James Connor, saved from the seashore by Police Sergeant Stockley, was carried to a hotel where he lay unconscious for eleven hours.

One who died despite making it to land was Boy First Class Bernard Arthur de Plumley Smyth. He had for many years been a chorister at Holy Trinity Church, Cuckfield in Sussex and joined the navy in 1913, aged 16. Plucked from the seas into the pinnace after *Formidable* sank, he collapsed and died upon landing at Lyme, a young life snuffed out when seemingly saved.

Further to the west, another fight for survival was taking place. The 34-foot cutter had been lowered and launched on the starboard side of *Formidable* but in the process most of the oars had been smashed. With great difficulty the seventy-one men on board managed to get clear of the sinking battleship before she sucked them down with her, and they used the remaining oars to keep the boat's head to the wind. For hours they were rowing incessantly and according to one sailor 'were so exhausted and suffering so much that we did not care whether we were rescued or not'.[9] The waves constantly threatened to swamp the boat and one young lad was thrown out into the sea by them where he remained for thirty minutes before he could be picked up. One bluejacket remarked, 'Quite sixty out of the seventy men took off their boots and used them as balers.' Another survivor said, 'We were baling all the time, and managed to keep the water under.'[10] They sang *Tipperary* but could not keep it up for long. It seemed that at the end of every line a giant wave would wash over them.

The boat became badly holed, and one man took off his trousers, stuffed them into the hole and sat on them to keep them in place. Dignity has no meaning in the face of death. The mast had been carried away so the boathook was pressed into service as a substitute and a black silk muffler attached to the top as a makeshift signal flag. One sailor clung to it like grim death for several hours to keep it erect. But their small vessel, battered by gale force winds and massive waves, continued to drift to the south and west until at approximately 9.30 am they were fifteen miles from Berry Head where providence intervened. They were spotted by a Brixham sailing trawler, the *Provident*, 75 feet long and weighing 50 tons, captained by William Pillar with his crew of three.*

Pillar, 30 years old, married and the owner of the *Provident*, was an experienced seaman and second coxswain of the Torbay lifeboat. He had participated in many rescues. Now he would face his greatest ever challenge. Captain Pillar had been running for shelter in the teeth of the gale and in mountainous seas, and had hove-to when his third hand, John Clarke, sighted the cutter. In flailing wind Clarke shinned up the rigging to get a better look and then reported to Pillar that there was a boat in trouble. As a lifeboat man, and a fellow sailor, William Pillar knew that he had no choice but to attempt a rescue. For him and for the survivors of the *Formidable* it was to be a defining moment.

As *Provident* approached the boat Pillar could see that it was full of water and leaking badly. He had to act quickly and in doing so he showed magnificent seamanship. With upmost difficulty he gybed his trawler and manoeuvred to windward, trying to get the cutter into the shelter of his lee. Eventually, after four attempts and nearly three hours of trying, he managed to get a line on board the little boat. Using his steam capstan, Pillar was able to haul the launch round to the trawler's stern, enabling the sailors to begin to jump on board. Constant waves, some thirty feet high, made the task both extremely dangerous and difficult. It took half an hour to get all the men onto the trawler, but he did it. Torpedo-Gunner Horrigan had been the senior man in the cutter and was the last to leave, clutching at the mizzen rigging to get himself aboard the fishing smack. Amazingly, only one man was hurt during the transfer, having jammed his fingers

---

*A Brixham trawler was a deep-sea sail fishing vessel built locally in the nineteenth century. There were once 300 of them operating out of Brixham harbour. They were characterised by their high speed and distinguishing red sails, which resulted from them being coated in local ochre for protection.

between the two boats. One young lad had to be carried aboard, no mean feat, as he was so weakened by exposure. Horrigan got off the launch just in time, for as he jumped on board, more dead than alive, the launch broke up and sank. If not for William Pillar, all seventy-one men would have been dead.

It is difficult at this distance to appreciate the skill and heroism displayed by the crew of the *Provident*. The local paper reported:

> With hardly a thought of the colossal risk the captain and crew at once set about rescuing the men in the boat. After a great struggle they managed to haul down the second reef of the mainsail and set the storm jib. The cutter, which had been riding at a sea-anchor rigged by the men, drifted towards the *Provident*, but in the mountainous seas they missed each other, and the naval boat passed out of sight of the men on the smack. For the moment they thought she was lost ... when made fast, the warp was coiled around the *Provident*'s steam capstan, and with great skill the cutter was hauled to a good berth astern. Then the warp was passed around the lee side, and the cutter was drawn up under the lee quarter.[11]

One survivor, Seaman Gunner Hughes, who had held the tiller for much of their ordeal, said of Pillar, 'I could not say too much in praise of that man.'[12]

The rescued men were in bad shape. Pillar later reported that they were in an exhausted condition, half of them having only flannels and shirts to cover them ('They were less than half-clad, indeed some of them were not covered by a shilling's worth of Navy clothing')[13]. An 18-year old boy, suffering from exposure, required immediate treatment on board to save his life. Pillar stuffed the men without trousers into the warmth of the engine room, and put the rest in the cabin and the fish hold. The trawler men pooled their food and cigarettes and divided them among their unexpected guests. Cook Dan Taylor was run ragged making coffee and other hot drinks.

But the fight was not yet over for Captain Pillar. He and his crew then battled for six hours through the horrendous weather, reaching Brixham at 1900. There he anchored in the outer harbour and rowed ashore to report the rescue to the coastguard and arrange for the tug *Dencade* – which gave a welcome tow – to help him reach the landing stage where the survivors were landed ashore.

Harold Smithurst had finally given in to the pain of his injuries and collapsed into the bottom of the boat where he remained awash until helped onto the *Provident*. Once ashore he was immediately dispatched to hospital and operated on for three hours. When told that an operation would be necessary he had replied, 'Better to have an operation than be lying beneath the deep blue sea.'[14] Boy First Class Eddie Wheatley, the swimmer, was another survivor. Private Mitchell probably summed up the view of all the men when he said, 'Our experience was terrible ... we were rowing for 11 hours to keep the boat's head to wind.'[15]

The local paper reported that 'the rescued men, who were in a pitiable condition, gave a hearty British cheer – the like of which only British tars could give – and sang "Auld Lang Syne", and then in batches of four and five wrapped in blankets, they were taken, by waiting cabs, to the Bolton Hotel, the Globe, the Cafe, the Sailors' Institute and Doidge's, these being the distributing centres.

'Here the men were provided with hot food and warm clothing and either went to bed at these places or went into private houses which were thrown open to them.'[16]

As the men came ashore, some immediately rushed to the Post Office to telegraph their families with the glad tidings of their survival. One matelot, trousers rolled up to the knee, flannel shirt topped by a lifebelt round his neck, stood to attention before walking to a waiting cab. 'Here we go again,' he intoned lugubriously. 'Undress uniform! Bathing costume!'[17]

Injuries were remarkably slight. Apart from Smithurst, one seaman had incurred an abdominal injury and another had injured his foot. Nine men were sent for further treatment including Petty Officer Second Class Harry Rumsey, in peacetime a coastguard, called up for the hostilities.** Pillar had saved them all. By his own words he had never seen a worse gale and thought 'it was a wonder that we were able to pick up any of the men'.[18] What he did when he had finally got the men to safety is not recorded. But he could be forgiven for taking a stiff drink, if not more than one.

**Rumsey did not benefit over long from his good fortune, dying aged 47 in 1921. His gravestone in St Margaret's, Leiston, Suffolk, records that he was 'severely injured in the sinking of HMS *Formidable*'.

7

Two Dogs and Some Funerals

Any man's death diminishes me because I am involved in mankind
And therefore never send for whom the bells tolls
It tolls for thee.

(John Donne, *Devotions*)

When the exhausted sailors from the pinnace were brought ashore at Lyme Regis the townspeople swung into action. The mayor provided the mayoral car for the worst affected to be taken to the Cottage Hospital. Some townsfolk took men to their own homes; others provided food and drink. When telegraphist George Wilson came round he found himself in a room 'being given brandy and hot soup and rubbed with towels by young ladies.'[1] The first thing he asked for was a cigarette. He was put in a motor car and taken to the house of a Mr Loud, who settled him in a warm bed. The local pubs were opened to provide shelter. One was the Pilot Inn, where the landlady was Mrs Atkins, and she volunteered the use of her cellar as a temporary mortuary.

The sailor who had tried to assist Sergeant Stockley, but ended up himself being rescued from the sea by the policeman, was Able Seaman John Cowan. Lying on the beach where Stockley had dropped him, he was barely dressed, cold, blue, inert, seemingly not breathing. The doctors

69

attempted resuscitation but gave up. Thinking him dead, they had his body carried to the Pilot Inn and placed with the other bodies in the cellar.

Like most pubs, the Pilot's publicans owned a dog, a cross-bred collie called Lassie. Collies are intelligent dogs, sheep-herders by breed, loyal and determined. This particular dog had also been trained to respond if the landlady collapsed, for she suffered a mild form of epilepsy. Little did Mrs Atkins know how these canine skills would propel her pet into a moment of fame. In the enquiring way of dogs, Lassie had wandered down to the cellar and over to where Cowan lay. She licked at his face and hands and then started to make whining noises. For some thirty minutes she continued to lick and nuzzle him until Cowan voiced a faint murmur in return. He was alive! Medical aid was speedily summoned and applied and the lucky sailor was rushed to the Cottage Hospital where over time he recovered.

The story had immediate appeal to a dog-loving nation in need of good news and the newspapers lapped it up. One wrote, 'Immediately willing hands completed the work the dog had begun and in a short time Cowan sat up. Since then the dog and Cowan have been inseparable and as Cowan is not yet allowed out, he and the dog spend most of the time before the kitchen fire cultivating the acquaintance so curiously begun.'[2] For Lassie too there was a happy ending. She was awarded two medals and was placed first in a special section at Cruft's Dog Show ('Spratt's Canine Heroes and Heroines') in the spring of 1915 (see also Appendix 1).

Captain Loxley's Airedale terrier Bruce also displayed loyalty and determination, but his fate was not as happy as that of Lassie. Loxley went down with his ship and Bruce died with him. Several days after the disaster, Bruce's body was washed onto the beach under Abbotsbury Castle, an Iron Age hill fort. His remains were buried in the pets' cemetery at nearby Abbotsbury Gardens with his own headstone. The inscription reads:

> BRUCE
> Airedale Terrier
> Who Stood Till The End
> With
> Captain Loxley R.N.
> On The Bridge Of
> HMS Formidable
> When Sunk By A Torpedo
> 30 Miles From Portland
> Jan 1st 1915
> +++
> Bruce's Body Was Washed Up
> Below Abbotsbury Castle

The American writer and dog breeder Albert (Bert) Terhune said of the Airedale terrier, 'He is swift, formidable, graceful, big of brain, an ideal chum and guard ... to his master he is an adoring pal. To marauders he is a destructive lightning bolt.'[3] Bruce's loyalty showed to the very end.

Abbotsbury beach was also the final destination for the remaining unaccounted for boat launched from *Formidable*. Pillar had saved the occupants of one, another had reached Lyme Regis, one had smashed on entering the water and *Topaze* had picked up another. The fifth was found below the castle by a party from the destroyer HMS *Savage*, bottom up, empty. Four bodies were recovered close by, so near, yet so far, from deliverance.

And on Monday, January 4th, two more bodies were washed ashore in Lyme Regis bay. Twins, the Villiers-Russell boys has been sick berth attendants on *Formidable*. Barely clothed they had died on board the pinnace, locked in each other's arms for warmth or comfort, and their bodies thrown over the side by the survivors to lighten the boat. Still gripped

71

together, their disfigured bodies came in on the tide like so much flotsam.

In memoriam, Lyme Regis

The coroner had convened an inquest at 1600 on January 2nd. No identity discs had been found on the dead men so Master at Arms Cooper formally identified them. Before the inquest closed, the coroner sent to the Admiralty asking for details of religion, age and given name in order that the men could be appropriately buried.

On January 5th, at the Baptist Church in Lyme, the congregation were moved to tears by the rendering of 'Fierce Raged the Tempest' (aka 'The Great Calm' by Revd Godfrey Thring) by Ordinary Seaman J.G. Saunders, one of the rescued. But the main remembrance by the town was the following morning.

It was a Wednesday. Lyme Regis turned out in force to commemorate the dead sailors. Shops closed, flags flew at half mast, floral tributes, including more than 100 wreaths, were displayed at the Assembly Hall. By the time of the funeral several thousand sombre-clad citizens lined the streets to pay their last respects and a great press of people filled the roadway below the west front of the church. At 1400 the procession began its way past the Buttermarket to the church of St Michael the Archangel, a sailors' church, set on the edge of a cliff overlooking the sea. An honour party of thirty men had been sent from the navy's Devonport Gunnery School. Lyme's Boy Scout troop lined the walk-way into the church. The church bells gave out muffled peals.

There were six coffins, each covered with the Union Jack. Preceding them in the procession was the Honour Party with reversed arms. A single coffin, containing the body of Petty Officer Feldon, was mounted on a gun carriage and the other five coffins were carried by local townspeople. A boy scout followed behind them carrying an oversize Union Jack and after him walked all forty-eight of the survivors from HMS *Formidable*, each carrying a single wreath. Then came a detachment of the 11th Battalion, Devonshire Regiment (a reserve battalion based in Exeter), the Mayor and Mayoress of Lyme Regis, mace-bearers with maces draped in black crepe, aldermen in their robes and town corporation officials. The Allied Nations were represented by Belgian refugees, housed in the town, who followed the procession, one carrying the Belgian flag, another the French Tricolour.

The Bishop of Salisbury, Frederick Ridgeway, the vicar of St Michael's, Canon Jacob, and other clergy from local chapels met the cortege at the entrance to the church. Ridgeway himself conducted the service. For the text of his sermon he took 'What the navy is doing'. He preached that there had been a lot of sarcastic newspaper comment about the performance of the navy. 'It would not do for the interest of empire that the movements of the silent navy should be public. England should be thankful that their homes are safe and not in ruins like Belgium.'[4]

The choir and congregation sang 'Let saints on earth in concert sing', Charles Wesley's hymn of quietus, and concluded with the organist playing Chopin's *Marche Funèbre* in C minor. As the final sombre notes rang out the procession reformed and proceeded up the steep hill to Lyme Regis cemetery. There the coffins were all laid in the same grave, a simple Celtic cross on a three-step plinth marking the spot at the very back of the old cemetery. 'Jesus Lives' was sung, the Last Post echoed across the gravestones and the honour guard fired a final salute to the deceased men.

Six sailors were buried there. Petty Officer W. Feldon, aged 36; Stoker W.C. Eley, 24; Stoker H. Bernthall, 19; Stoker W. Fawkes, 31; Stoker H. Souter, 27; and Boy 1st Class B.A. de P. Smyth, 17. The stokers would have been stripped to the waist, working in the boiler rooms. They had little chance against the wind and cold so dressed.

As they walked back from the church some men spoke of revenge. But for one, Signalman E.H. Merton, there was time to reflect on his outrageous good fortune. In the space of five months he had been sunk and rescued three times – on HMS *Amphion*, HMS *Cressy* and now *Formidable*. His fairy godmother was working overtime, although some thought he must have shot an albatross.

The good burghers of Lyme Regis had done right by the men of *Formidable*. Among other gestures, all the survivors had been made honorary members of the local Liberal Club which allowed them access to beer and pastimes, and Wilson had been taken on a motor drive by his host, a new experience for the telegraphist. The secretary of the hospital measured the men's feet for new boots and the Mayoress of Exeter sent new underwear. The men recognised the kindness they had received. One man stated, 'I did not believe that there were such kind people in the world.'[5] Another named his daughter 'Phyllis Regis'.

When the time came for the surviving sailors to leave, on January 8th, Leading Seaman Thomas Carroll presented the mayor with the ship's crest (it now hangs in Lyme Regis Guild Hall) as a token of their appreciation for the townspeople's kindness and hospitality. Then they marched to the railway station for the 0920 train to London, accompanied by the town band and cheering residents. The mayor made a valedictory speech in which he wished them all the very best for the future – a future they very nearly didn't have. As the engine pulled out of the station the band continued to play, whistles were blown and the fog signals by the railway tracks were let off. They left behind three of their number, still confined to hospital. One was Cowan, the other two were boys, Albert Goole and Francis Shee.

Arriving in Chatham the survivors were met on the

platform by relatives and family. Hardened sailors broke down and cried. Some despairing kinfolk had arrived hoping that the casualty lists were wrong, and they now stood listless and silent in the background. Then the men boarded their transport to barracks where they were issued new kit and given ten days' leave. It was over.

In memoriam, Brixham

Brixham was a long-time seafaring town, a fishing port with over 300 sailing trawlers in 1914. Its citizens were well aware of the power of the sea to wreak destruction and loss on those who dared to challenge its dominion. As the plight of the *Formidable*'s survivors became known the townspeople knew what to do.

The rescued men were housed in private homes and local hostelries, and seventeen of them at the Fisherman's Institute, where they were looked after by Miss Burney, cousin to Ballard's father-in-law. Brixham's womenfolk bought beds and bedding for them; the wife of the vicar of nearby Paignton, Mrs Fuller, sent warm clothing; the Royal Naval College at Dartmouth provided refits, motored over by an officer and ratings.

On Saturday morning Lady Leith and Miss Burn (the local MP's daughter) visited the men while Lord Leith of Fyvie (a former naval officer who had received the Royal Humane Society's medal for rescuing a boy from drowning) called on Captain Pillar to express his admiration. And on Sunday about fifty survivors attended divine service at All Saints Church where the curate, Reverend Acheson, led the prayers. The congregation sang the hymn 'Abide with Me', written nearly 100 years previously by the then parish priest of All Saints, Henry Francis Lyte, while he lived at Berry Head House, commanding a view of the very seas from which the men had been rescued.

Monday came and those men who were fit enough began their journey back to normality and Chatham barracks. Warrant Gunner Horrigan and Boatswain Taylor paraded the men at the Town Hall where the deputy leader of the council gave an oration (the leader, Reverend Sim, was indisposed having just learned that his only son had been killed on the Western Front). The National Anthem was played. The men gave three cheers to the town and the crowd responded in kind. Many of *Formidable*'s men embraced and kissed the young Dan Taylor. And then they marched off to Churston station for the 1040 train to London. That evening Brixham Urban Council met and moved a vote of sympathy with the relatives of the men who had lost their lives in a 'national calamity'. And the following day the fishermen resumed their fishing and the fishwives their gossip. For them too, it was over.

In memoriam, Crewe

It was raining as the London and North Western Railway train drew into Crewe station at 2210 on January 5th, 30 minutes later than expected. There was a large crowd, reckoned at over 1000 souls, gathered to await the arrival, the homecoming, of the bodies of the Villiers-Russell twins.

They had left Lyme Regis that morning in a special van, first via the London and South Western Railway to the capital and there transhipped to LNWR for their final journey home. There was some further delay while a goods van was manoeuvred into position next to the parcels office. Two wooden coffins with elaborate brass mountings were tenderly lifted by the assembled bearers into two hearses, black, dark and damp in the glow of the street lights. Men bared their heads. A line of the Civic Guard snapped to attention. Police under

Superintendent Thompson did the same. As the coffins slid into the hearses a floral tribute in the shape of an anchor was placed on top. And then the mournful procession, escorted by Civic Guard and police, and followed by a large number of people, set off through the artificially lit streets of Crewe. It was, according to the local paper, 'weird and saddening'.[6] Another report stated that 'the spectacle was a unique and impressive one in the lurid glare of the street lamps and it evoked upon all sides a sympathetic attention'.[7]

As the cortege passed through the Market Square, a clock chimed eleven. Outside the Primitive Methodist church in Henry Street there was another large crowd. As the hearses drew up, there were whispered asides of sympathy. Once again the bearers lifted the coffins and carried them into the chapel. 'The room was nearly full of sympathisers and there was a hushed expectancy.'[8] The circuit minister offered a prayer for Divine comfort, especially for the widowed and now son-less mother. 'Many people present found it hard to restrain emotion and smothered sobs were heard among the people.'[9]

The interment took place two days later at two in the afternoon, but long before that time a huge crowd had gathered. It had rained in torrents but the citizens of Crewe were undeterred. Their boys had given their lives in patriotic duty and it was Crewe's duty to give honour in return. Crewe was a single-employer town: the railway works. Everybody knew everybody. This was a communal loss.

The day before, the coffins had been covered with Union Jacks, but they were now completely smothered in flowers sent from friends and town institutions. They were placed before the communion table and the Reverend C.L. Tack began the burial service. He delivered a moving eulogy. The twins were, he said, 'lovely in their lives. Their devotion to one and other was remarkable.'[10] They were 'true patriots [who] believed in philanthropy and universal benevolence ...

they were generous in their moods, in their love and in their chivalry ... their lives were consecrated to a sacred service.'[11] 'Forever with the Lord' and 'Jerusalem my happy home' were sung. The church was packed and over a thousand people waited patiently outside as well. The mayor and corporation were there, off duty soldiers, ambulance men, nurses, the Crewe Brotherhood, the Loyal Crewe Lodge of Oddfellows.

At the conclusion of the service, the cortege re-assembled for their final journey to Coppenhall church. Again thousands of people lined the route and 'with all their power bestowed sympathy on the poor lonely mother'.[12] Despite the rain, heads were uncovered as the procession passed. Blinds were drawn in every house, flags flew at half mast, shops closed in respect. The rector conducted a second service and then the bodies were laid to rest in two graves, dug either side of their deceased father's grave, and covered with thirty wreaths. 'Jesus lover of my soul' was sung. Men cried. Two buglers played the last post. It was still raining.

So, with patriotism and honour, Crewe buried its dead. The town would lose another 698 men before the war was over.

The tragedy of the *Formidable* did not end at the beginning of January. The trawler *Rhodora*, out of Ramsgate, trawled in a body of a seaman and recommitted it to the deep, not knowing of the sinking as they had been at sea the whole time.

On 9 January the trawler *Varuna*, sailing from Brixham and fishing fifty-five miles SE of Berry Head, pulled in its nets to discover a body in the catch. The body was dressed in a blue jersey, flannel shirt and a pair of canvas trousers on which a name tag identified the corpse as 'A. Chantrell'. Naval Reserve Stoker Alexander Chantrell had just turned 18 the previous month and had served on *Formidable* since being called up on August 2nd 1914 from his job as a sheet galvaniser at the iron works in Stockton-upon-Tees.

Able Seaman George W. Ashbee's body was washed ashore in France, at Dieppe, on February 4th. On 5 February the bodies of Private William Bennett and Stoker Frederick Mead were discovered near Burton Bradstock and buried in that village's churchyard. The next day the corpse of 17-year-old signal boy Frederick Norman was found ashore at Charmouth and identified by his flotation collar. His body was claimed by his parents.

And sometime later another body was washed up on the shore at Seatown, near Chideock. The inquest decided that it must be from *Formidable*. The unidentified corpse was interred in St Giles' Churchyard, Chideock, with full military honours and at a later date a wooden cross was erected over the grave with a brass plate attached and inscribed:

JESU MERCY
In Memory Of An Unknown Man
Claimed By The Admiralty As From HMS Formidable
Washed Ashore Feb. 12th 1915

The headless corpse of Private William Bennett came ashore on the coast, again at Burton Bradstock. It was identified by the clothing tags. And on the 18th, in West Bay, a headless and handless body came ashore, still wearing a blue jersey, flannelette shirt, blue web belt and service pattern boots; the letters AJC in white on the jersey identified Pte Alfred Joseph Clapham from Kings Cross.

And still the suffering continued. On 23 February the trawler *John Donovan* brought in a body; it had 'A. Norams' on swimming collar but F.N. Baker on a knife and keys. A frightened matelot taking another's floatation aid? Possibly, but there was no 'Norams' reported as in the crew. The body was identified as Ordinary Seaman Frank Nixon Baker, 29. His father obviously cared little for his dead son. He telegraphed from the Isle of Dogs that 'it was impossible for me to go [to collect the body] ... his religion is CofE'.[13]

In all, the loss of life on *Formidable* was 583 men from a complement of 780. Out of 75 boys, 58 were lost; from 14 midshipmen, 8 died. The majority of the dead never found a grave. Sadly, unlike his dog, Captain Loxley's body was never recovered. Neither was that of his second-in-command, Commander Charles F. Ballard, son-in-law to Admiral Burney having married his daughter Violet in 1913. His loss was particularly poignant; on January 8th the 'births and deaths' column of his local newspaper carried the following announcement:

BALLARD Dec. 29, at 8 Royal Crescent, Weymouth, the wife of Commander Charles F. Ballard, R.N., of a daughter.[14]

The little girl would never know her father.

Of the 197 men saved, 48 were rescued at Lyme Regis, 71 by Captain Pillar, the remainder by the light cruisers. *Diamond* accounted for all the surviving officers and midshipmen (ten in total), including the senior officer to survive, Engineer Commander C.J.M. Wallace, who sustained a broken rib which required hospitalisation. The grief naturally felt by the survivors was perhaps not aided by the reported comments of the skipper of the fishing ketch *Our Laddie*, Captain Adams. His was probably the nearest ship to the *Formidable* but he claimed that neither he nor his crew knew the meaning of the lights being shown by the ship. 'I could have saved the whole lot,' he observed when he learnt the truth. 'I never for one moment thought they were signals for assistance.'[15]

What made the death toll even more tragic was that the losses could have been fewer had the Admiralty listened to concerns about its life collar, which as Stoker Taplin's account confirmed was more hindrance than help and totally useless in storm-tossed waters. The *Sydney Morning Herald* commented that 'a large proportion of those saved were wearing patent inflatable waistcoats which are spoken of as being more efficient than life-belts'.[16] Rather than being open to new ideas and dealing with questions raised in the House of Commons, which unfavourably contrasted the British equipment with that used by the Germans, the Admiralty continued to champion the collar. It said it was easy to carry, did not encumber the wearer in the performance of his duties and was an efficient aid to swimming.

But officers were not convinced and opted to buy the Gieves waistcoats, which further called into question the Admiralty's belief in the efficacy of the swim collar. For example, Lieutenant Stephen King-Hall, writing to his parents on 7 January 1915, states, 'I have thought about the Gieves waistcoat, several people on board have got them, they are expensive, but the prevalence of mines and submarines have influenced me to order one. The North Sea is rapidly becoming no place for yachts!' And in a later letter to his father he pleads, 'Will you hurry Gieve up with my waistcoat? You might point out over the telephone that a gentleman in a Light Cruiser is more likely to test its powers than someone in a guardship. However, no need to tell Mother this.'[17]

Events surrounding the sinking of HMS *Hampshire* in 1916 (with War Minister Field Marshall Kitchener on board) simply made the case even stronger. Many bodies washed ashore wearing the swimming collar were found to have suffered broken necks, caused by the action of the collar when they jumped into the water.

Some weeks after the sinking, a lifebelt from *Formidable* was washed up on the Dutch coast, having made its lonely voyage across the North Sea. The Dutch stored it in Magazine Kattenburg, Amsterdam. It was later handed over by the Dutch authorities to Captain S.C. Manning, who presented it to the Imperial War Museum in June 1920, the year it opened to the public. It is a small but permanent remainder of the suffering of January 1st.

Recognition and reward

Recognition for the heroism displayed during the sinking of the *Formidable* was mixed. For William Pillar and his crew it meant a visit to Buckingham Palace. For his outstanding gallantry he was awarded the Board of Trade Sea Gallantry Medal for bravery by His Majesty King George V, as were his three crewmen. The king, himself a career navy man until the death of his elder brother had cut his service short, told Pillar, 'I congratulate you upon your gallant and heroic conduct. It is indeed a great feat to have saved 71 lives. I know myself how arduous it is to gybe a vessel in a heavy gale.'

There were also awards from the Admiralty – £250 for Pillar, £100 each for crewmen William Carter and John Clarke, and £50 for the young boy, Daniel Taylor. This was a substantial purse (worth perhaps £22,000, £9,000 and £4,500 respectively today) at a time when the average agricultural labourer earned around £40 per annum (see also Appendix 2).

The Devonshire Association also recognised Pillar's bravery. On 30 January 1915, while the event was still in everyone's minds, the Association (founded in 1862) gathered in London to present Captain Pillar with an illuminated address. It was a sizeable event involving many local dignitaries and the presentation of the address was made by George Lambert MP, who was Civil Lord of the Admiralty and Liberal member for the Devonshire constituency of South Molton.

The committee of the Shipwrecked Mariners Association also showed their appreciation, awarding the Society's Gold Medal to the skipper, with a purse of £5, and the Silver Medal and a purse of £3 to each of the other members of the crew, publicly bestowing the awards in Brixham Town Hall on February 13th.

The teenaged apprentice and cook, Dan Taylor, featured in a book called *Child Heroes of World War One*. Taylor also received a ten-shilling postal order from an admirer in Hampshire, and a Paignton resident sent a shilling for 'the kind boy Dan who did his best'.

Brixham itself was not to be left out of the acclaim for Pillar, and a 'People's Fund' was established for subscriptions to honour Pillar's crew. Local MP Colonel Burn sent an immediate contribution of five guineas and over £200 was raised in total, the equivalent of some £20,000 today.

Pillar himself received many letters of appreciation. One was from the Mrs E.J. Hughes, the mother of Gunner Hughes whom *Provident* had rescued. She wrote from Belfast, 'Thank you for your noble and brave deed in rescuing my dear son and others. Words cannot express my feelings for your kindness. My heart is too full for words. How I wish that I could see you to thank you for your kindness to my dear boy ... May God bless you and yours.'[18]

A 6-year-old child wrote, 'My Dear Captain Pillar. I hope you are very well. How brave you were saving those men, and I hope you get a V.C. Love from Edward Corcoran.'[19]

For Pillar himself the adulation was more of a trial than the rescue. A shy and modest man, he found his new found prominence an ordeal. When presented with the Shipwrecked Fishermen and Mariners' medals he commented, 'We only did our duty as every Englishman would do and I think that every Brixham Fisherman would do the same.'[20]

Nonetheless, the influential 'clubland' evening newspaper the *Westminster Gazette* gave Pillar and his men this encomium: 'They may rest assured that their splendid seamanship and gallantry have won them a secured place in the record of

Great Deeds in the Great War. They kept cool and were British in Captain Loxley's inspired words of injunction.'

Leading Seaman Thomas Hanlon Carroll, the man credited by many of the Lyme Regis survivors with getting them safe to shore, received no decoration in recognition for his struggle with the elements. But he was immediately promoted to Petty Officer in rank, the navy equivalent of a sergeant in the army, which, as it brought more in wages and benefits, might have been a more desired reward. Gunner Daniel Horrigan, senior man on the boat rescued by *Provident*, received an 'expression of Their Lordships Appreciation', conveyed personally by the Commander-in-Chief Nore, the popular Admiral Sir George Callaghan.

The example of Bugler Reed's courage was raised in the House of Commons by G.F. Hohler (the Member of Parliament for Chatham) and as a result the Admiralty sent a letter of appreciation to his family. Reed was also awarded the Royal Humane Society's Life Saving Certificate and an anonymous poem about his self-sacrifice was published in many newspapers. Written in six deathless verses it ended:

> The drum – the drum of England!
> Oh, it makes us very glad.
> You parted with it to your friend
> Brave little bugler lad.

Police Sergeant James Stockley was awarded the Silver Medal of the Board of Trade for Gallantry and the Bronze Medal of the Royal Humane Society. He was also awarded the Carnegie Hero Fund Bronze Medal, that institution's highest award, together with the sum of £20 and an entry in their illuminated Roll of Honour, housed in the Carnegie Birthplace Museum, Dunfermline.

For Tom Walker, his near death experience in the cold waters of the English Channel proved too much for his constitution. There was no promotion or citation for mere survival and he was discharged as 'medically unfit for Naval Service' in April 1915 with an 'Honourable Discharge' certificate signed by King George V.

And on the other side of the Channel the cause of the disaster, Kapitänleutnant Rudolph Schneider, also received due recognition. Unlike his colleague Otto Weddigen, he was not awarded the *Pour Le Merite*, the German equivalent of the British Victoria Cross, an award requiring 'extraordinary personal achievement'. But he did receive the Iron Cross First Class the day after his triumph and the *Hausordern von Hohenzollern mit Schwertern* followed in November.

PART II

Invictus

In the fell clutch of circumstance
I have not winced nor cried aloud.
Under the bludgeonings of chance
My head is bloody, but unbowed.

(W.E. Henley, *Invictus*)

8

Après le Déluge

Every why hath a wherefore.
(William Shakespeare, *The Comedy of Errors*)

'The loss of the vessel is in itself no very serious matter, as the whole history of the fighting by sea in this war goes to prove the enormous superiority of ships of more recent construction, and the decision will be arrived at ultimately by ships not more than ten years old. It is however, quite otherwise with the loss of life, which is to be regretted in itself but also for its bearing on the question of the manning of the fleet. It takes many years to make a seaman of the type who went down with the Formidable. Certainly those men cannot be replaced during the present war.'[1]

The disaster of the loss of the *Formidable* had both causes and consequences, as did the behaviour of the officers, sailors and civilians involved. They inhabited a world in which there were many more certainties than we might observe today. There were expected forms of behaviour, established hierarchies, predictable situational responses and an innocent acceptance of whatever life threw up. Life was fairly binary, wrongs and rights clearly perceived, views expressed in black and white.

True there were undercurrents of resentment and change.

89

The years leading up to the war had seen large-scale and sometimes violent industrial unrest including dock and railway strikes and a vast coal strike. The first seven months of 1914 included over a thousand strikes or walk outs and 9.9 million man days were lost. But on the whole the Britain which, haltingly and without much forethought, went to war in 1914 was one in which flourished an age of prelapsarian delight.

The navy had changed little since the time of Nelson. It had not fought a major battle in 100 years and its pre-war tactical doctrine was still largely locked in a discipline that Nelson would have recognised; close engagement, broadside to broadside firing, admirals directing the manoeuvres of their fleets with unbounded wisdom and authority. That this doctrine changed on the very eve of war under pressure of *materiel* and circumstance was a further challenge to the often limited intellectual resource of the navy's top brass. The way in which senior officers had been raised and trained, in the blessed 'Vicwardian' era of unbounded empire, was limited and limiting and, in rendering them intellectually sterile and inflexible, did not equip them well for modern warfare. The root of the disaster of *Formidable* and other such losses lay in this flaw.

At sea and on land there were expected behaviours for Englishmen whether of military or civilian persuasion. The stiff upper lip, stoic acceptance of danger and abnegation of self were all tropes of the age, and are what come to mind now if we try to imagine the character of that time. But in fact these were relatively recent behavioural stereotypes in 1914, the product of the later Vicwardian age and its cultural obsessions and thought leaders. They were inculcated through literature and art, education and peer example. Loxley and Ballard were as much prisoners of these norms as were the sailors who served under them.

The loss of the *Formidable* was a national loss. Its

ramifications were felt across Great Britain and its Empire. Previous naval wars had relied on men largely impressed from the major sea-ports of the south coast and the losses in men had impacted mainly in such towns. But the call up of reservists and the patriotic rush to volunteer made the sinking of the old lady something which had national impact, and families the length and breadth of Britain felt the pain. Coupled with the growing realisation of the staggering losses being sustained on the Western Front, this called for a proactive response from government to counter a growing feeling of unease and disillusionment. Propaganda made its debut in modern warfare and *Formidable* played her part.

The end of the war left many people with unresolved grief and what would now perhaps be called post-traumatic stress disorder. A focus for national and local grief was needed. Slowly at first and then with increasing frequency, war memorials began to spring up like dragons' teeth across the country. By the late 1920s there was hardly a town or village which did not possess one. And the dead of *Formidable* found themselves immortalised in stone and marble, a last whisper of their existence captured for their relicts to ponder and remember by. For families and friends left behind, and for the survivors of the sinking too, there was no return to Eden. Britain after the war, broke, exhausted, unmodernised, politically split and very different from the confident Britannia that had entered the war, was a challenging place to re-engage in normal life.

As the following chapters in Parts II and III will show, like wraiths *Formidable* and her crew touched all of these issues. She might have gone to the bottom in 1915 but she and her men, the quick and dead, remained unconquered. They did not let Britain down – it was Britain that let them down.

9

To Be an Admiral

He thought so little, they rewarded he
By making him the Ruler of the Queen's Navy.
                    (W.S. Gilbert, *HMS Pinafore*)

The navy was not stocked with many capable or competent admirals at the outbreak of war. Jellicoe, Beatty, Hood, Trywhitt, and possibly Keyes might be remarked upon and remembered even today as excellent commanders, but there were many more who did not inspire confidence. Milne has already been met and dissected; Burney, the previous incumbent of Bayly's seat, was in chronically poor health, slow, conservative and had little in the way of imagination. Warrender, who suffered from deafness and absent-mindedness, was thought to be a good commander but was found in practice not to excel in any regard. Both these men were responsible for battle squadrons in the Grand Fleet. Jellicoe's second in command (and also his wife's brother-in-law) Madden lacked imagination and was a plodder. Leveson, Director of Operations at the Admiralty, was a bully, and Sturdee, the Chief of Staff, thought he knew all there was to know about warfare and would take no counsel from anyone else. Bradford and Gamble, who also commanded squadrons under Jellicoe, had 'never revealed any creative powers or willingness to use the brains of their subordinates'.[1] De Chair, who was in charge of the Tenth Cruiser Squadron on the Northern Patrol, was a lovely man but was neither 'an inspiring leader or a strong character'.[2] Grant, in charge of the Sixth Cruiser Squadron and the senior cruiser admiral afloat, was 'a mediocrity'.[3] And so on. How did this come to pass? Why, when the time came for the navy to demonstrate its Nelsonian élan, was the human *materiel* so lacking?

The Vicwardian navy was a club. And like most clubs it had rules about who could join. The minor aristocracy, the land-owning squirearchy, younger sons of the nobility – this was the core membership profile. Eldest sons of the aristocracy went to the army or parliament before inheriting their father's estate and titles. Younger sons joined the church or the navy. Once in the club it was important to follow the rules. If one did so, promotion would inevitably follow. If not, 'troublemaker' status would ensue and it was a long and lonely road to advancement. The pivotal rank was that of commander. Commanders were generally second in com-mand of large ships, a sort of chief operating officer, responsible for presenting the ship to the captain as a going concern. But it was not warlike qualities or excellent gunnery that would bring a commander distinction. A smart ship, bright paintwork, gleaming brass, cleanly dressed crew, unquestioning and speedy attention to orders – these were the qualities that were looked for. It helped to have a private income, for commanders frequently paid out of their own pockets for extra paint and gilding or even uniforms. Spon-sors helped too. Loxley had served as staff-commander to two admirals, Callaghan and Milne, and both had worked hard to advance his career.

If successful, promotion to captain followed. To be a captain afloat was to be a sort of demi-god. Able to come and go as you please, in sole authority over hundreds of men, with a secretary and personal servants, a private cabin and dining arrangements – it was a position of immense privilege and power. A captain came aboard his ship to the shrill, quavering notes of the boatswain's pipe. Marine guards snapped to the 'present'; officers uncovered heads. A marine sentry guarded his suite, which often contained the only proper bath on board. The captain was not addressed until he made the first approach. He had power and dominion over advancement, discipline; he was a benign (or otherwise) despot. And once a captain it was very likely that flag rank would follow, as a strict principle of seniority ruled (for example, Bayly was promoted to Rear Admiral in 1908 on the retirement of Rear Admiral Reynolds).

Royal connections helped. Both Edward VII and George V maintained a keen interest in the navy through their lives – indeed George served, reaching the rank of commander before the death of his brother, the heir to the throne, in 1892 propelled him into retirement and the succession. Both kings interfered in the appointment of admirals and captains on occasion (as has been seen in the affair of Admiral Milne, see Chapter 2) and service with royalty, or on the Royal Yachts, was a ticket to influence and promotion. As examples, on the outbreak of war Milne commanding the Med was a 'royal' appointment. Meux, CinC Portsmouth, was only there because George V had wanted him to be First Sea Lord but Churchill demurred and, under pressure, gave him the second prize. The Second Sea Lord, Admiral Hamilton, was a royal favourite through the influence of his wife. Burney had been Aide-de-Camp to Edward VII in 1906, Madden in 1910; and, indeed, Bayly in 1908. Warrender's second child had Queen Victoria for a godmother and Battenberg, the First Sea Lord, was married to one of Queen Victoria's granddaughters. Rear Admirals Christian and Campbell, both 'royal' admirals, were jointly responsible for the disaster of the 'live bait squadron' (see Chapter 4). Et cetera.

When flag rank was attained, a flag officer could have

authority over thousands of men and millions of pounds of weaponry, and the life and death of both friend and enemy lay in his hands. He made and unmade careers from the lowest sailor to the highest-ranking subordinate. He was possessed of plenipotentiary powers, and while abroad on service represented the monarch and government. In the far flung corners of the world, away from communication with London, flag officers made and unmade foreign policy. The flag officer was the Supreme Being wherever he went, so much so that Admiral 'Pompo' Heneage refused to kneel for divine service in his naval uniform, as a British admiral did not recognise a superior – Pompo always changed into civvies for such events.

Flag officers had personal servants, their own barge and crew, a suite of officers to fulfil their every desire or order and untrammelled authority over their ships and captains. Their orders were unquestioned, divine writ, omniscient and omnipotent. The fact that nobody chose to question Bayly's orders and dispositions on the night of December 31st 1914, although many were pleased to criticise them *post hoc*, is but one example of this characteristic. And if no admiral was present then this mantle of power fell to a commodore or senior captain afloat.

The navy was a complacent, arrogant world, sure of its own authority and greatness. To be an admiral or senior captain was to gain the publicity attendant on footballers today. *Vanity Fair* featured drawings of you. Newspapers wrote of your exploits and opinions. The tropes of the navy – dreadful sailor suits for children, full-set beards, smoking – became fashionable. Sailors and the navy featured in advertising for popular goods such as cigarettes and alcoholic drink. The Navy League had nearly 2.5 million members.

And so generations of admirals grew up in a world where, educated in the navy from the age of 12 and frequently serving for long periods abroad, they had very little contact with modern society or culture. They inhabited a world of unquestioning obedience to orders and where societal skills and attention to detail were more rewarded than warlike or command-based qualities. They lived in a closed system which closely resembled the one they had left behind in England where their fathers and brothers ran the country.

This was the milieu that bred 'Luigi' Bayly. Fisher's reforms of 1904, in which he tried to improve the navy's 'gene pool', education and fitness for war, had begun to have an impact on the younger officer class, but it was too late for those who would command in 1914. For better or for worse, men personally brave but collectively ignorant would be in charge. Vice Admiral Sir Lewis Bayly was but one such.

H.M.S. FORMIDABLE.

THIS ILL-FATED BATTLESHIP SANK IN THE ENGLISH CHANNEL AFTER A TERRIBLE EXPLOSION IN THE EARLY MORNING OF 1st JANUARY, 1915. A TERRIBLE GALE WAS RAGING, AND ONLY 199 OF OUR BRAVE SAILORS WERE SAVED OUT OF ABOUT 750. THE GALLANT CAPTAIN BEING AMONGST THE DROWNED.

Top: Postcard of HMS *Formidable* with (insert) Captain Noel Loxley.

Above left: Leading Seaman 'Micky' Carroll at Lyme Regis (reproduced by permission of Lyme Regis Museum).

Above right: Able Seaman John Cowan (and Lassie) at Lyme Regis (reproduced by permission of Lyme Regis Museum).

Above: Formidable Funeral Oration, Church of St. Michael the Archangel,
   Lyme Regis (reproduced by permission of Lyme Regis Museum)

Below: Formidable communal grave, Lyme Regis

Above: Bruce's grave, Abbotsbury Gardens

Below: A typical Brixham fishing smack

HMS *Formidable*
before the war

Admiral Sir Lewis Bayly

10

The Culprit

If you are out to beat a dog, you are sure to find a stick.

(Yiddish proverb)

The Admiralty had been uncertain as to whether it was a mine or a torpedo that sank *Formidable* and some naval experts suggested that 'the gale possibly dis-anchored some mines laid eastward of Dover causing them to drift down the channel'.[1] The Great British Public did not find out that it was a submarine attack until January 3rd, when British newspapers reproduced an official statement from the German navy. It ran: 'On January 1st, at three a.m. one of our submarines, as it reports by wireless, torpedoed and sank the English battleship *Formidable* in the English Channel, not far from Plymouth ...' The truth was out. Now a culprit had to be found.

Vice-Admiral Lewis Bayly had taken command of the Channel Fleet on December 17th 1914, replacing Burney who went to the Grand Fleet, and had sailed with the Fifth Battle Squadron as its direct commander on December 30th. He had previously been in command of the First Battle Squadron of the Grand Fleet. Aged 57 at the time of appointment, Bayly had been in the navy all his life, joining the training ship *Britannia* at Dartmouth in July 1870 at not quite 13 years of age, and was the great-great nephew of

Admiral Sir Richard Keats (who had achieved prominence at the Battle of Algeciras Bay).

Bayly's career had followed the usual progression with service at home and abroad, including the Ashanti Wars of 1875 and the Egyptian campaign of 1882. He reached the rank of captain on New Year's Eve 1899. His captain on his last ship before this elevation had been unwilling to recommend him for promotion, so Bayly went to see the First Sea Lord, Walter Kerr, whom he did not know, in person and adumbrated to him the reasons why promotion should be his. Luigi Bayly (his nickname within the navy) was known as a 'character'. Hard, tough independent, he was a stern disciplinarian who did not suffer fools gladly. He gained an early reputation for running a 'tight ship'. In 1906, when he was captain of HMS *Queen*, Admiral Bridgeman wrote into Bayly's Naval Record, 'Ship is exceptionally clean, organisation excellent, ship as a whole is a credit to the service'; and Admiral Lord Beresford added at a later date, 'Was second ship in British Fleet at battle practice, is a model of what a British man-of-war should be.' However, some thought that he 'extracted good service from his subordinates because they were afraid of him'.[2]

He attributed his success to 'working a minimum 11 hours a day, never smoking before 10pm, walking at least 20 miles on Sunday, playing tennis for an hour at 0630 and running round Greenwich park at 1730.'[3] A keen student of naval history, he had a reputation for being a great tactician and had conceived the use of smoke screens for tactical purposes.

He was also opinionated and stubborn. In 1900 he had been appointed Naval Attaché to the USA and Japan. His successor, Dudley de Chair, noted that 'he had been recalled, owing to his rather indiscreet conduct there'.[4] Certainly he had been recalled because the American Secretary of State (John Hay) had written to the British Ambassador that he would like Bayly to give up the job.

Eventually Bayly achieved Flag Rank in 1908 and was appointed to command the Royal Naval War College. His predecessor, Rear Admiral Edmond Slade, told Admiral King-Hall that 'he did not think Bayly a good choice'.[5] Admiral Jellicoe, commanding the Grand Fleet, was also no fan of Bayly's. Discussing the choice of commander for the First Battle Squadron in 1916 he wrote, 'I don't think Bayly will do. He had such curious fits of heroics and he proposes such impossible things that I doubt his judgement now.'[6]

He was, however, an aggressive commander and this endeared him to First Lord of the Admiralty Winston Churchill. When Bayly was in charge of the First Battlecruiser Squadron in 1912, 'Churchill would come to Portland almost every weekend and he and Luigi Bayly would go for long walks hatching plans for new exercises. The result was that at 2.00 a.m. on Monday we would raise steam and put to sea until the next weekend. The guns were constantly firing and the coal dust made a fog on the mess decks.'[7].

His association with Churchill continued when in 1913, after he had handed the First Battlecruiser Squadron over to Beatty, he was seconded to the Admiralty to work on Churchill's pet project of landing on and taking over the island of Borkum, one of the East Frisian islands off the coast of Germany, to be used in case of war as a base for close blockade. This idea was not adopted and did not command respect.

Bayly and Churchill appeared to be developing a more than professional relationship. On 27 January 1913 Bayly had written to Churchill to thank him for arranging for Bayly and his wife to attend the parliamentary debate on the navy estimates and for giving them dinner afterwards. Luigi noted, 'I am sure the service will be proud of its representation.'[8] In this he was perhaps gilding the lily, for he must have known that many in the navy felt the opposite. Writing again to Churchill at the end of the same year, after he had been made a KCB (Knight Commander of the Bath), Bayly effused,

'You have been very good to me and I am most grateful both personally and in so far as I may be considered to represent the service.'[9]

On 22 February 1914 Bayly wrote again to Churchill from his Third Battle Squadron flagship HMS *King Edward VII* to thank him for his appointment to the more prestigious First Battle Squadron. He again noted, erroneously, 'You have the service behind you as one man as far as we seagoing people count,' adding, 'Keep the people across the North Sea quiet till July, then, as soon as you like.'[10]

Churchill was often guilty of having 'favourites' and clearly Bayly had achieved this prized position himself. And the First Lord was not alone in his opinion. Prime Minster Herbert Asquith thought Bayly 'one of our better officers'.[11] Marder considered him 'an able tactician with a mania for discipline and efficiency'.[12] Certainly he seemed to glory in his 'hard man' image. On becoming Commodore (T), he had 'told the First Lord (Lord Tweedmouth) that the destroyers would be worked night and day and I did not expect to lose more than one every six months'.[13]

Bayly was reputedly never known to smile and when at a later date he was commanding a mixed force with American ships, the Yankee sailors named him 'Old Frozen Face'. He had married in 1892, to Yves Henrietta Stella Annesley Voysey, cousin to the famous architect C.F.A. Voysey. She was seven years his senior and had been married once before. There were no children.

This, then, was the man who had presided over the loss of the *Formidable* and was now to be held responsible for it.

Condemnation was not long in coming from all sides. Captain Herbert Richmond at the Admiralty (as assistant director of operations) spoke for the majority in his diary entry of January 4th: 'It looks like some lunacy of Bayly's. So I should expect it to be. The man has no judgement, is as obstinate as a mule and is too stupid to convince.'[14]

Fisher was particularly angry. He wrote to Churchill on January 6th, 'It must have been patent to every officer and man in his squadron that to steam at slow speed in close order on a moonlit night on a steady course in the vicinity of Start Point was to make his squadron an easy target to the hostile submarines which all the precautions taken by the Admiralty to escort him from Sheerness must have convinced him was a very present danger.'[15]

Jellicoe, to whom Bayly had reported until taking command in the Channel, refused to take sides. Writing to Churchill on January 10th he commented of Bayly that 'his many fine qualities you know too'. However, he went on to add that 'he is sensitive and somewhat of a poseur'.[16] Churchill was unconvinced, replying the following day that 'he has outraged every principle of prudence and good seamanship without the slightest military object'. But then he added, in a comment that suggests he might have being trying to self-rationalise a more lenient treatment for his quondam protégé Luigi, 'I am grieved about Bayly. I am doing my best for him, not for his own sake but because to terrorise Admirals for losing ships is to make sure of losing the war.'[17]

The abuse of the admiral continued to spread, even reaching the ears of His Majesty's representative in the Hague. Sir Allan Johnston, Minister to the Netherlands, wrote to Churchill to pass on the contents of a letter written by a relative of his who lived in Weymouth. Concerning Bayly, the relative commented that the general view among the naval officers to whom he spoke was that he was 'a chap with superabundant energy and no brains. When he commanded the battleship squadron he nearly produced a mutiny and the lower deck call him "the murderer".' The letter went on to assert that 'the officers are full of criticism of the Admiral ... they say he committed all possible faults coming along much too slow and in a long line ... Sir Louis [sic] Bayly has always been unpopular in the service.'[18]

Fisher meanwhile continued to fulminate. Writing again to Churchill on January 14th, he fumed, 'He has lost our confidence and that is sufficient reason for his removal and no other reason should be given him! When you give your housemaid warning – however excellent she may be – you don't have to explain. You don't like her so she goes.'[19]

Commander Kenneth Dewar, a naval 'brain' and iconoclast, was on board HMS *Prince of Wales* with the Fifth Battle Squadron during the events of January 1st. A specialist in tactics, a leading light in the *Naval Review* magazine and a future Director of Plans at the Admiralty, he was critical of the old fashioned ways of the navy. Writing to a fellow officer after the event he stated, 'I do not think it would have been possible to take greater risks than were taken on that night.' He continued, 'there is no doubt that *Formidable* was sacrificed to the gross stupidity of a very ignorant man – and long before the incident occurred both officers and men criticised the folly of taking such risks for no reward whatsoever. One does not blame the Admiral – he is God – the Navy made him – a thoroughly obstinate and stupid man. One blames the system which makes it possible for such a man to command a fleet ... no one thought he would be employed again until Winston Churchill gave him command of the 3rd Battle Squadron.'[20] Even junior officers were forthright in their condemnation. Lieutenant King-Hall, writing to his parents from HMS *Southampton* at Rosyth, noted, 'The loss of the *Formidable* appears to have been very unfortunate. They were in close order, and only going 6 knots! It is scandalous no Nelson has arisen yet.'[21]

What made the loss of the ship and so many good lives appear all the more regrettable to the Admiralty and the public was that it appeared to have been due to taking risks for no good purpose. The usual course of action in any loss of vessel would be to hold a Court of Inquiry (see Appendix 3). But further publicity was the last thing the Admiralty wanted at the time. Its record of poor management was causing considerable concern at all levels of government and in the press, and Churchill's position (never entirely safe as he was generally not trusted by his colleagues) was under threat. And such Inquiries had a habit of rebounding badly upon Churchill and his Sea Lords.

After the escape of the *Goeben* (see Chapter 2), Rear Admiral Ernest Troubridge had been arraigned before a Court of Inquiry which found that he had failed to 'pursue an enemy then flying' and recommended he be court martialled. This took place in early November 1914 but, to the astonishment of many, he was found not guilty. Instead, implicitly, the Admiralty were blamed for confused, and confusing, orders and the press (and some MPs) began to agitate for better explanations.

Following the disastrous loss of the three 'Bacchante class' cruisers in September (see Chapter 4) the Admiralty were again blamed for poor dispositions. A Court of Inquiry was set up and found that some blame was attributable to all of the senior officers commanding the cruisers. But the bulk of the opprobrium was directed at the Admiralty for persisting with a patrol that was dangerous, of limited value and against the advice of senior seagoing officers. Both the Third and Fourth Sea Lords added their weight to the criticism of the conduct of the Admiralty.

In late October the First Sea Lord, Battenberg, the executive head of the navy – ill with gout and overwork, attacked viciously by the press for his German ancestry and tired of his subservient relationship with Churchill, his boss – asked to be allowed to resign, seemingly suffering a nervous breakdown. Churchill replaced him with the ageing Fisher (now 73) but this was not received well in all quarters, the king, for example, protesting strongly and delaying the appointment.

Then on November 1st Rear Admiral Sir Christopher 'Kit' Cradock, leading a significantly outmatched British squadron of scrapyard ships against a crack German squadron, and tired of being told by the Admiralty and by Churchill personally that he had the means to attempt the task of destroying the German vessels, was lost, with two of his ships and over 1600 men at the Battle of Coronel. Churchill tried to place the blame on Cradock and misrepresented both his orders and *materiel* to parliament but the press were 'onto it' and difficult questions regarding the Admiralty's role were being asked. Indeed, retired Admiral Lord Charles Beresford (an MP and no friend of Churchill's) wrote to Admiral Sir Frederick Hamilton, 'the Navy will lose confidence in its leaders if officers and men are murdered without any particular object'.[22]

Consequently the last thing the Admiralty and its First Lord wanted was another public airing of dirty washing. So they settled for severely censuring Bayly for his perceived mishandling of the battle squadron and for not taking measures to avoid submarine attack. Bayly immediately asked to be court martialled in order to have the opportunity to formally clear his name, the example of Troubridge no doubt foremost in his thinking, but this was refused and he was eventually replaced by Vice-Admiral Bethell on January 17th. Prime Minister Herbert Asquith wrote to his amorata Venetia Stanley, 'Winston tells me that they have recalled Lewis Bayly from the command of the Channel Fleet as a consequence of his loss of *Formidable*, & have put Admiral Bethell in his place. It is rather disquieting, for Bayly was supposed to be almost the pick of our younger Admirals. Bethell, whom I used to see on the C.I.D., is to my thinking no flier. We really seem to have better reserves in the way of Commanders in the Army than in the Navy.'[23]

For his own part, Bayly blamed the Admiralty. In his autobiography *Pull Together* he stated that he was ordered to turn back the destroyers after passing Folkstone. He marshalled his defence. 'Judging by this order and by the daily reports of the known or supposed position of enemy sub-marines in the western half of the channel I took the fleet down towards Start Point.'[24] In other words his defence was that 'nobody told me!' He went on, 'I asked for a court martial and was refused – I have never known why. It sounds like a fairy story, seeing what happened during the war, and pre-sumably was done to encourage other Admirals.'[25] No sign of regret or remorse then, or later, apparently. However, he tried to remain philosophical. 'It is well to remember that in a disciplined force an essential of that discipline is facing injustice with a smile,' he wrote.[26]

His friendship with Churchill certainly seemed to have helped Bayly for while he did not get the court martial he craved, shortly after his defenestration he was appointed President of the Royal Naval College, Greenwich, a largely ceremonial and administrative post and possibly a way of keeping him 'warm' until matters had died down.

In the House of Commons Churchill played an increasing swell of questions regarding the incident with a straight bat. He had previously told the house (on 27 November 1914), after the blowing up of the *Bulwark*, that Great Britain could afford to lose a super dreadnought monthly for one year and yet maintain the same superiority that she held at the out-break of war. Now he was attacked in both the press and the house for the seeming minimisation of the loss of *Formid-able*. The *London Daily News* of January 2nd commented, 'It would be idle to pretend that the loss of the *Formidable* is not a serious blow to us,' and went on to add, 'Whatever the value of the ship, her loss is of far less importance than the loss of 700 officers and men ... they were all picked men ... expensively trained.' The *Morning Post* weighed in too: 'It is useless to pretend that this is a small matter,' it thundered.

On February 4th William Joynson-Hicks, Conservative MP for Brentford, questioned Churchill:

Mr. JOYNSON-HICKS; asked the First Lord of the Admiralty whether the Fleet of which the *Formidable* was one was cruising without attendant destroyers, and, if so, why; and whether this was the first occasion on which they had so cruised under a new admiral?

Mr. CHURCHILL; I cannot undertake to discuss the conduct of naval operations during the progress of the War.[27]

On February 8th Sir C Kinloch-Cooke, MP for Devonport and therefore with a strong interest in naval maters, also quizzed the First Lord:

Sir C. KINLOCH-COOKE; asked the First Lord of the Admiralty whether he can give the House any further information concerning the sinking of His Majesty's ship *Formidable* than was contained in the announcement made public at the time of the event, when it was stated, on the authority of the Admiralty, that it was not certain whether the vessel was struck by a torpedo from a submarine or a mine?

Mr. CHURCHILL; As stated by my Noble Friend Lord Crewe in another place, the definite opinion of the Admiralty is that His Majesty's ship *Formidable* was sunk by two torpedoes fired from a submarine.

Sir C. KINLOCH-COOKE; asked the First Lord of the Admiralty whether he will explain to the House on what duty Admiral Sir Lewis Bayly's squadron was engaged at the time of the sinking of HMS *Formidable*; whether any inquiry or court-martial has been held; and, if so, whether it is proposed to make public the result?

Mr. CHURCHILL; Sir, I do not think there is any advantage to be gained by the discussion of this matter at the present time. It is not proposed to hold any formal inquiry nor to bring any person before a court martial. The Board of Admiralty have considered attentively all the circumstances and I have no statement to make.[28]

Bayly was not to get his day in court and the Admiralty's dirt would remain under the carpet. But he was not to be underemployed for long, for Churchill certainly held him in high regard. By July he was appointed Senior Naval Officer,

Coast of Ireland, in charge primarily, and a perhaps little ironically, of anti-submarine warfare – although by then Churchill had himself been forced out of his job too.

11

The Admiral and the Admiralty

> *Let a man accept his destiny*
> *No pity and no tears*
> (Euripides, *Iphigenia in Tauris*)

The outline of the Admiralty's action against Bayly, and his defence of his dispositions, have been considered in Chapter 10, but the detail is important and deserving of closer examination. After all, the sinking of the *Formidable* was a human disaster and, following as it did a number of similarly catastrophic losses in which the dead hand of Admiralty interference or mismanagement had been publicly alleged, the First Lord (Churchill) and his Sea Lords were keen to point the finger elsewhere, openly and without hesitation. And Luigi Bayly was keen to protect his good name and reputation.

The Admiralty wrote to Bayly on January 11th, via the Permanent Secretary to the Navy, Sir William Graham Greene, uncle to the future novelist. They blamed him squarely for the loss of *Formidable* and made three key points. First, Bayly was criticised for keeping the squadron at sea for a 24-hour period in an area and at a time when 'as you must have been fully aware, the English Channel was infested with enemy submarines'.[1] Second, they noted that 'the

direct consequence of your prolonged stay in these dangerous waters was that the enemy's submarines were afforded
ample opportunity to locate your squadron'.[2] Finally, the
Admiralty were concerned at the slow speed of the squadron,
its close formation on a straight course and the positioning of
the light cruisers astern. 'These dispositions,' the letter
rumbled on, 'were such that your squadron offered an easy
target for the submarine attack which resulted in the loss of a
valuable ship and the irreparable loss of the lives of 600
officers and men.'[3]

The Lords Commissioners of the Admiralty thus decided,
they informed him, that they could form no other conclusion
than that 'the handling of your squadron for the period in
question was marked by a want of prudence and good seamanship in the avoidance of unnecessary risks, inexplicable
in an officer holding high and responsible command'.[4] The
letter continued, 'The facts ... affect your position most seriously but, before taking a final decision [the Lord Commis-
sioners] are willing to receive any statement you may desire
to make in explanation of your actions in this deplorable
event.'[5]

This was a very severe reprimand and it no doubt stung
Bayly's pride – and what is more it put his professional career
in the balance. He responded in writing from his flagship,
HMS *Lord Nelson*, two days later. His rebuttal was fierce. He
averred that not a single submarine had been sighted in the
channel since he had hoisted his flag and there was thus no
evidence to suggest that the channel was 'infested' with
submarines. This was of course disingenuous, for he had only
been in command for fourteen days at the time and as
detailed in Chapter 4 there was plenty of evidence of submarine activity around the east coast of Britain and into the
Dover Straits prior to his appointment. However, he did have
a telling point, which was that the Admiralty daily schedules
of movements of German ships was blank for the Channel 'in

every copy I have here'.[6] But of course, the whole point of a submarine is that it is hidden!

Luigi went on to claim that, as the Sixth Battle Squadron had just exited the area without reporting any submarine contact, his assumption was justified, and he suggested that the Admiralty should have told him if they knew of enemy in the area. He stated that 'I therefore had no information whatever as to the presence of any submarines in the channel; and there was nothing to lead me to suppose that any very special danger existed.'[7] This rather seems to discount the fact that Britain was at war with an enemy known to possess an active submarine fleet.

Regarding his destroyers, to which, of course, the Admiralty had not referred, he stated that they had turned back at Folkestone under Admiralty orders (actually to escort the returning Sixth Battle Squadron) and therefore the Admiralty knew that he did not have an anti-submarine escort with him. Bayly also took the opportunity to blame the Admiralty for the fact that he had neither light cruiser not destroyer flotillas attached to the Channel Fleet, a subject on which he had already corresponded, as had Burney, as they both believed that such measures were necessary.

As to the other points of criticism, Bayly noted that the squadron's average speed was 12.5 knots, that the sixteen-point alteration of course after dark, in line with section 177 of Channel Fleet orders, had been conducted at 19 knots, and that his decision to steam in close order (incidentally the preferred option for most pre-war manoeuvres) was justified, for if spread out the squadron would have given an enemy submarine a better chance of obtaining a shooting position. He claimed that in this case perhaps two vessels would have been lost – lost to a submarine he did not believe to be there, that is. As for a straight course, he averred that he had never undertaken zig-zagging at night (this was probably true, for the navy was very reluctant to do anything at night, including fight or practise firing, unlike the German navy) and had only steered a straight course between 1900 and 0300 anyway. Referring to Channel Fleet and Grand Fleet orders, which specified the speeds and nature of the turns he had made, he suggested that as these had been promulgated by officers senior to himself, he was justified in following them without modification or addition. Once again, in the navy the divine omniscience of authority manifests itself.

Regarding the cruisers, in a rather sophisticated piece of reverse logic, Bayly argued that if they had not have been at the rear the loss of life would have been greater, as nobody would have seen *Formidable* hit and her wireless had been disabled.

The Admiralty were nonetheless unmoved and he was ordered by a telegram of January 16th to haul down his flag the next day, as he had lost Their Lordships' confidence. Given that a Court of Inquiry had not been convened, on February 4th Bayly requested a court martial to clear his name and reputation. As was outlined in Chapter 10, this was the last thing the Admiralty wanted. Their Lordships were unmoved and unconvinced. They wrote to him at the Royal Naval College on February 10th with two bitter pieces of news. First they confirmed that 'in consequence of the circumstances consequent upon the incident in question you had lost Their Lordships confidence and therefore you were directed to haul down your Flag',[8] and second, that 'their Lordships are not prepared to admit that an officer had a right to demand trial by Court Martial and they are not prepared to accede to your request'.[9] And so Luigi simmered at Greenwich with his tail between his legs and his reputation sullied. For a hard, unyielding career seaman this was a hard row to hoe.

Within the trail of correspondence above there is one mystery. The letter of condemnation sent to Bayly on 11 January is two pages long, and was no doubt painful enough to him. The original of the letter lies in the Admiralty files at Kew. However, there is another letter, headed 'January' but with no actual date, which is six pages long and is coruscating in its sustained criticism of Bayly's actions off Portland. It bears the unmistakable sulphurous stamp of Fisher's invective. This letter lies in the Churchill manuscripts at the Churchill Archive Centre, Cambridge. In the letter's final section there is a clue that Bayly was neither regretful nor remorseful about the loss of *Formidable* and that either from bluster or a genuine belief in the righteousness of his defence (or just because that was the way he always behaved) he had failed to show the Admiralty the appropriate humility. Paragraph five of six states, 'I am further to draw your attention to your personal demeanour which, on the two occasions when you were summoned to the Admiralty since taking your new command, has been improper and unusual. ... whether from a surfeit of bravado or from ill-temper; whether they are involuntary or affected; I am to warn you that they are to be changed and changed radically at once.'[10]

This letter is unsigned and is not the letter that was actually sent. Did Churchill intervene to water down this draft, keeping it in his voluminous files? Was it for reasons of friendship or for self-protection? Part of the answer may lie in a minute from Greene dated 12 January 1915 and circulated to the First Lord and Sea Lords. Again it lies in Churchill's papers at the Archive Centre. In it Greene notes, 'I think the Admiralty tacitly concurred in his [Bayly] keeping his squadron at sea for tactical exercises for a day or two.' In other words, 'Watch out, this could rebound on us again'. That Bayly gained no court martial and was rebuked but not severely punished is possibly explained by this short note.

Rehabilitation, resentment and retirement

Bayly's period on the naughty step did not last long. In July 1915 he was recalled from Greenwich to take command of the Western Approaches, based in Queenstown, Ireland, commanding a mixed force of sloops and Q-ships (disguised ships heavily armed but masquerading as merchantmen) to prosecute anti-submarine measures. In 1916 he was made CinC and played a role in the suppression of the Easter Rising. When the USA entered the war in 1917 Bayly took overall command of some ninety-two US ships, as well as British ones, and worked well with the American forces for the duration of the war, earning their respect and admiration. He was promoted full Admiral on 3 November 1917 and eventually retired from the service on 1 April 1919, laden with honours; these included the KCB and KCMG, Danish Grand Cross of Danneborg, United States Distinguished Service Order, French *Legion d'honneur* and the Order Crown of Italy. He had had a good war.

The Americans held him in high esteem and he received a letter of commendation from Franklin D. Roosevelt, Assistant Secretary of the Navy; forwarded by 'Force Commander, US Navy forces', it read, 'The Department believes that, without exception, the feeling towards Ad Bayly of all United States Naval officers who have served during the war, either ashore or afloat, from the Queenstown base is not only unusual but unprecedented in the Allied warfare.'[11]

But the blame attached to him for the *Formidable* affair still rankled with Bayly. He wanted satisfaction. In March 1919, just before his retirement, he wrote to the Admiralty asking that the case be re-opened with a view to 'justice being publicly done'[12] and in order that the official history of the war, being prepared by Sir Julian Corbett, should correctly reflect his role.*

---

*In fact Corbett attributed the loss as follows: 'In this particular instance the disaster was attributed to the neglect of ordinary precautions.'

In this letter, written from his base in Queenstown, he included all previous correspondence and noted once again that it was the Admiralty which had ordered the destroyers to leave him at Folkestone, a fact that he clearly saw as having grown in importance. It is indeed possible that he was by now being blamed for sending them away himself; certainly there are some accounts of the sinking which say he did, erroneously.

The matter of Bayly's letter was discussed at the Admiralty Board of April 17th but no one saw any reason to oblige him, and some good reasons not to, not the least that an Inquiry now would set a precedent which could lead to many more such cases.

Once again, his application was rejected. The Admiralty wrote to him at his home in Ermington, Devon, on April 25th. They pointed out that as, under Section 54 of the Naval Discipline Act, more than three years had elapsed since the incident they were precluded from re-opening the case, and added that they did not feel justified in questioning the decision of a previous board.** But they did reiterate the sentiments of fullest appreciation of his services previously expressed in the consolation prize they had sent him on April 5th for his efforts as CinC at Queenstown. In that document, the Lords Commissioners of the Admiralty conveyed 'their appreciation of the manner in which you have carried out the important duties of that command and their satisfaction with the very high standards of efficiency maintained by HM Ships and Naval Establishment under your orders'. They concluded that 'your services have been of great value towards the successful prosecution of the war'.[13]

For Bayly, fine words buttered no parsnips. Determined and tough, single-minded and proud as a commander, he was

---

**It is interesting to note that the file relating to the Bayly and the Admiralty's correspondence was marked 'closed until 2020' in 1919, and only cleared for reading in 1993. Somebody had wanted the file buried completely.

not about to yield when retired. On May 1st he replied to the Admiralty in fulminating tones and scrawled handwriting. He railed that the Admiralty had not been 'unable' to accede to his request for a court martial, they were 'not prepared to'.[14] He dismissed the Section 54 argument with the comment that 'it only forms an excuse for not holding one'.[15] He concluded that 'it therefore appears that their Lordships consider it to be more just for an individual officer to be very severely punished unheard, than for a previous board decision to be re-opened'.[16]

Although Bayly was not to know it, behind the united front presented by the Admiralty to his request for a re-opening of the case there were some with sympathy for his plight, and who thought a greater injustice lay beneath the surface. When Bayly's letter of May 1st was circulated to the Board, the Deputy Chief of Naval Staff (DCNS) felt obliged to comment on it. His perspective is of interest, for the DCNS was Rear Admiral Sydney Freemantle, the naval prosecutor in the court martial of Rear Admiral Troubridge in the *Goeben* affair (see Chapter 2). In a handwritten note dated May 9th he wrote, 'I do not know if it is the intention to discuss this matter at a Board meeting – I cannot put all I should like to say on this subject on a circulating paper. I will, however, go so far as to say that I think the degree of blame which might be attributed to Admiral Bayly in <u>1915</u> is open to question; the decision to refuse his request for a Court Martial at the time most regrettable; and the tone and expression of some or most of the letters written to him by the then board still more so. I do not question the correctness of the view now taken, in any way, but I should welcome any solution which would remove the sense of injustice from which Admiral Bayly is suffering' [the underlining is in the original].[17] So Freemantle thought Bayly hard done by, and that blame might lie elsewhere. Did he see or know that Churchill and Fisher had been desperate to allocate blame solely to Luigi? What did he not wish to say in a 'circulating' paper? In private, did he point the finger of blame in another direction?

The Second Sea Lord read the memorandum on May 12th. He suggested to the First Sea Lord (Rosslyn Wemyss) that they obtain the First Lord's (Walter Long) consent to agenda it at a board meeting. Wemyss agreed. On May 13th he noted, '... there are several circumstances connected with the case which are regrettable, but I see no way of rectifying them. I am of the opinion that in spite of Admiral Bayly's protests, the original decision must be adhered to.'[18]

But they could find no way out of their difficulties. The Admiralty board considered his missive on May 22nd. Their answer remained unchanged. Bayly could not resist a bitter final note; on May 28th he scrawled back, 'My final experience in the Navy is that of injustice shewn [sic] to me by my official superiors.'[19] There was no reply.

Bayly's resentment no doubt marred his retirement to some extent. But, unlike the dead of *Formidable*, he was at least able to enjoy it.

Reconciliation

Bayly's animus stayed with him; and in particular his antipathy to Churchill, whom he had regarded as a friend, had supported and felt had deserted him. However, three years before his death he met Churchill at the 1935 Spithead Silver Jubilee Fleet Review. It was a magnificent occasion with 160 British navy ships present, and all the great and the good from the past war had been invited. Luigi was now an old and failing man but discovered that he and Churchill could still connect. Afterwards he wrote to his onetime First Lord that he 'had hoped never to see or hear from him again' but having met him at the recent naval review he was writing to pay tribute to Churchill for his role in forming the fleet. He went on, 'I write this because the bitterness has passed and I greatly regret that the great part you played in bringing the fleet up to its splendid strength in 1914 was not fully recognised. You need not answer this.'[20] But answer it Churchill did, writing on July 23rd from his home at Chartwell, 'I have never harboured any feeling about you other than those of severe respect and admiration ... I must always regard you as a comrade.'[21]

Luigi Bayly died, perhaps a little appeased by Churchill's letter, just under three years later in May 1938.

12

The Captain Went Down with the Ship

Courage is a kind of salvation.
(Plato, *The Republic*)

Captain Loxley went down with his ship. In the best tradition of the naval mythscape he was seen to walk to the side of the forebridge, light a cigarette and, his faithful dog at his side, await the end. But why does the captain go down with his ship? What example or doctrine requires him to do so? And why did Noel Loxley so decide?

There are legal considerations dictating a captain's behaviour at the time of crisis and, while these were probably not at the forefront of Loxley's mind when the *Formidable* went down, they nonetheless have some bearing on how a captain is expected to act. In maritime law the responsibility of the ship's master for his ship and his passengers, if any, is paramount, no matter what the vessel's condition. Abandoning a ship therefore has legal consequences, including the nature of salvage rights. Even if a captain abandons his ship in distress, he is generally responsible for it in his absence and is required to return to the ship when danger has passed. In the navy if a captain evacuates a vessel in wartime it can be regarded as a serious offence on a par with desertion, mutiny, or sedition, unless he destroys the ship or contrives that it sinks. It is for these legal reasons that a captain is often the last to leave a sinking ship and the first to re-board it, where possible.

But there is a stronger, cultural imperative, one forged in the crucible of Vicwardian education, self-perception, imperial grandeur and societal expectations. The dominant moral codes of the Vicwardians were derived from their reverence for the chivalric, the lost Eden of Arthurian legend, Camelot, the Round Table and for their obsession with England as a new Rome. The educational system was founded on the classics. The ancient Greeks and Romans were seen as great exemplars to imitate, their legends and myths as modern moral codes to be followed. And of course there was a strong religious element to the chivalric – the Christian ethic of love and self-denial, of putting others before one's self. Old Squire Brown in *Tom Brown's Schooldays*, when despatching Tom to (public) school says, 'If he will only turn out a brave, helpful, truth telling Englishman, then gentleman and Christian, that's all I want.'[1]

Chivalry and self-sacrifice, unspoken love and yearning, the pursuit of ideals and good deeds, the placing of women on a pedestal – these were the tropes of the age. The seminal novels were books such as Charlotte M. Yonge's *The Heir of Redcliffe* (where the hero bears his trials with Christian fortitude and sacrifices his life in nursing his no-good cousin back to health). In poetry Tennyson's *Idylls of the King* (1859–73) or the works of Swinburne (especially *Laus Veneris* – where Tannhauser believes that through pursuing physical love he has been banished from spiritual love – and *The Leper*) were role models; Malory's *Mort D'Arthur*, Le Motte Fouqué's *Sintram* (the wild knight desiring to be the epitome of a courtly knight and resist his lust for his guest's wife) the historical models. In art a plethora of Galahads, Lancelots, Guineveres and Arthurs decorated studios and drawing rooms alike. Burne-Jones's *The Death of Arthur in*

Avalon, one of the grandest and, in his view, the defining painting of his long career, was the Arthurian apotheosis. H.E. Luxmore, a master at Eton, Loxley's alma mater, gave his favourite departing pupils copies of G.F. Watts' painting *Sir Galahad*. John Percival, headmaster at Clifton College, christened his sons Arthur and Lancelot. In every boy's room at Eton there hung a copy of a painting of the disaster at Majuba Hill by Lady Butler. It depicts an officer with uplifted sword charging towards certain death with the cry *Floreat Etona*! ('May Eton flourish').

More prosaic popular figures were Henry Newbolt, whose poem *Vitai Lampada* ('They Pass on the Torch of Life'), published in 1892, became a shorthand for the times ('There's a breathless hush in the close tonight, ten to make and the match to win' and 'Play up! Play up! and play the game'), Sir Walter Scott and W.E. Henley. Scott in particular was responsible for evoking an age of personal honour, selfless courage and a romantic view of the protective feudal relationship through novels such as *Ivanhoe* (published as early as 1820). William Morris was another powerful influence, his prose romance *The Well at Worlds End* (1896) – a tale of young Prince Ralph in search of the redemptive and healing well at the end of the world – was read by virtually every literate man in England immediately before the beginning of the war.

The chivalric code also governed the Victorian approach to personal bravery. In schoolrooms all over the country the texts were Hector and Achilles, Horatio and the bridge, Arthur and his knights, Childe Roland, Prince Rupert, Moore at Corunna, Nelson at Trafalgar, Gordon and the Dervishes. Captain Lawrence Oates's self-sacrifice in Scott's ridiculously amateurish attempt on the South Pole (beaten by the more professional Amundsen who knew ruefully that Scott, with his death, would be the one to be remembered) was held up in hundreds of books as an exemplar of chivalric and

Christian courage. When, in January 1914, the trustees of the British Museum accepted from his widow the original of Scott's polar journal, the director, Sir Frederic Kenyon, was moved to write that the document would 'do much to enforce the lesson which was often in Captain Scott's mind during the latter days of his great march, the lesson that men of English race can face death without flinching for the honour of their nation'.[2] Such examples and sentiments were no doubt uppermost in the mind of Aeneas Mackintosh, Ernest Shackleton's number two on Shackleton's 1914–17 Imperial Trans-Antarctic Expedition. In February 1916, marooned in the ice fields and expecting to die, he wrote a poignant farewell message which echoed Scott's stoic self-sacrifice. He message concluded, 'If it is God's will that we should have given up our lives then we do so in the British manner as our tradition holds us in honour bound to do. Goodbye, friends. I feel sure that my dear wife and children will not be neglected.'[3]

Henry Newbolt's *The Vigil*, published on the day war broke out, probably earned him his knighthood. He later wrote that 'our airmen are singularly like the knights of old romances. There is something especially chivalrous about these champions of the air.'[4] It was no surprise that in 1914 reports of the 'Angel of Mons' or the Agincourt bowmen seen helping British soldiers on the Western Front were accepted as truth, and claims that German soldiers had been discovered killed by arrows were credulously accepted. The young poet Rupert Brooke wrote five 'war sonnets', published in *1914 and other poems*; they are drenched with words such as honour, glory, sacrifice, heroism and a mythical idea of 'England'. The third sonnet contains the line 'Honour has come back, as a king, to Earth'. Published in May 1915, a month after his death while serving with the RNVR, the poems clearly caught the zeitgeist, being reprinted twelve times by January the following year.

Indeed poetry, a last flowering of English romanticism, had an explosion of popularity at the onset of the First World War. In August 1914 *The Times* was receiving more than one hundred verses per day from the general public. They favoured four- or eight-line stanzas with a regular metre and were full of words such as 'bold', 'valiant' and 'pure', with symbolism using flags, swords and helmets. The poetastic efforts in praise of the men of *Formidable* and of Loxley which are quoted in Parts I and II of this book are but small examples of the output, and poetry clearly touched a nerve as a release valve for the pent-up patriotism and sense of passionate grief in the country.

Between 1860 and 1880 games had become a compulsory part of the curriculum in all major schools. Edmond Warre, headmaster of Eton in the later part of the nineteenth century, was a particularly strong advocate for them, believing that only through sport could he inculcate his desired values of fortitude, public spiritedness, measuredness in victory and firmness in defeat. At the outbreak of war many rugby union clubs signed up their members en masse. *The Times* of 24 November 1914 took to poetic encouragement, printing verses that overtly joined together the tropes of religion, self-sacrifice, duty and sport in one piece of doggerel:

> Come leave the lure of the football field
> With its fame so lightly won
> And take your place in a greater game
> Where worthier deeds are done ...
> Come join the ranks of our hero sons
> In the wider field of fame
> Where the God of Right will watch the fight
> And referee the game.

Association football, on the other hand, kept on playing. The FA Cup final took place on 24 April 1915 between Sheffield United and Chelsea at Old Trafford, and it was only with the

126

greatest reluctance that the Football Association decided to cancel tournaments for the duration. Presenting the cup to Sheffield, who won, Lord Derby (the cabinet minister responsible for armed forces recruitment) told both teams to 'play with one and other for England now'.[5]

But if Arthurian romance and Greek myth were the artistic and literary models for Victorian chivalry, then cricket was its sporting metaphor. The public schools had embraced cricket as the only game for gentlemen, and games between Eton and Harrow, for example, were watched and reported on in a fashion resembling an Ashes clash of later years. A game of laws not rules, of self-sacrifice to the needs of the team, of respect for umpires and fair play, an amateur sport where professionalism had a lower rank and status, cricket defined the Edwardian era. Loxley would have imbibed this in his brief years at Eton, and thousands of young and impressionable youths would have instantly recognised the link between bravery on the cricket pitch and self-sacrifice on the battlefield implicit in Newbolt's *Vitae Lampada*. Indeed one writer thought that Newbolt had been responsible for the creation of *Homo newboltiensis*, 'honourable, stoic, brave, loyal, courteous'.[6]

Hubert Preston, editor of the cricketers' almanac *Wisden* wrote of the 'chivalry of the playing fields of Harrow'.[7] At the outbreak of war these schoolboy cricketers marched instinctively off to the Front, but many saw no need to curtail the cricketing activities at home. *Wisden* railed against those 'spoilsports' who wanted to close the game down. 'In these grim times, losing Surrey v Yorkshire might be a necessary sacrifice – but the Varsity match? Unthinkable!'[8]. However, the grand old man of English cricket, W.G. Grace, saw things differently. Writing to *The Sportsman* on 27 August, three weeks after the declaration of war, he asserted that it was 'not fitting that able bodied men should be playing day by day and pleasure seekers should look on ... I should like to see all first class cricketers of a certain age set a good example.'

E.W. Hornung, author of the *Raffles* books and himself schooled at Uppingham, wrote:

> No Lords this year, no silken lawns on which
> A dignified and dainty throng meanders
> The schools take guard upon a fierier pitch
> Somewhere in Flanders.

His only son was to die at Ypres in 1915.

For another *Wisden* editor, Sydney Pardon, 'Cricketers' and 'the public schools' merged into a single sterling model of all that was brave and fine about the English character. 'Cricketers have made a splendid response to the call to the colours,' he wrote in 1915. In the same year, at the MCC's annual meeting at Lords, Lord Hawke, President, proposed a toast to the fact that three quarters of first class cricketers were in the army or navy.

By the war's end Siegfried Sassoon was mocking such sentiments. In his poem *Dreamers*, he wrote:

> I see them in foul dug-outs gnawed by rats
> And in ruined trenches lashed by rain
> Dreaming of things they did with balls and bats
> And mocked by hopeless longing to regain
> Bank Holidays.[9]

But the public schools kept the faith. Eton alone lost 1,000 former pupils, 20% of those who served. At King's School, Worcester, they inscribed the cricket pavilion with the words 'In Memory of those who, having learnt in this place to play the game for the school, played it also for their country'.

So Loxley, and indeed all of his peers, would be soaked in a cultural marinade that saw self-sacrifice as both noble and desirable. When the *Audacious* went down, Admiral Bayly was one of the last to leave the ship; but he commented,

'Captain Dampier followed me, he being the last to leave, according to tradition.'[10] It was a behavioural norm.

But the roots of this form of chivalry's application to the sea are quite shallow. The seminal event seems to have been the wreck of the *Birkenhead* in 1852. On February 26th, while transporting troops to Algoa Bay, she was wrecked at Danger Point near Gansbaai, 140 kilometres from Cape Town, South Africa. There were not enough serviceable lifeboats for all the passengers, and the soldiers famously stood firm, thereby allowing the women and children to board the boats safely. The ship was stiff with soldiers, including the 75th Regiment of Foot and the Queen's Royal Regiment, but their discipline was superb. Only 193 of the 643 people on board survived (the ship's captain, Robert Salmond RN, went down with the ship), and the soldiers' chivalry gave rise to the 'women and children first' protocol when abandoning ship.

The bravery and chivalry of the soldiers was immortalised in popular culture. *The Times* called it an act of 'matchless chivalry'.[11] Rudyard Kipling wrote a poem 'Soldier an' Sailor Too', immortalising the phrase 'Birkenhead drill' which came to describe courage in face of hopeless circumstances. Samuel Smiles drew attention to it in his bestselling book *Self-Help*.* It featured in popular paintings too (for example 'The Wreck of the Birkenhead', c. 1892, by Thomas Hemy**). All of

---

*Smiles referenced the *Birkenhead* when writing about character and the essential qualities of a gentleman. Referring to the cry 'women and children first' he observed that 'the examples of such men never die' and noted the upright way in which the soldiers and sailors went to their deaths.

**Thomas Marie Madawaska Hemy (1852–1937) was a marine and coastal painter who worked in watercolour and oils. He was born on the passenger ship SS *Madawaska* while his family were en route from Newcastle upon Tyne to Australia. After two and a half years in Australia they returned to Newcastle before later moving to North Shields. Hemy himself spent several years at sea and endured a shipwreck.

these representations highlighted the valour of the men who stood at attention and played in the band as their ship was sinking, and held up such behaviour as exemplary.

Other examples soon followed, such as Captain William Lewis Herndon who, in September 1857, was in command of the commercial mail steamer *Central America* when she encountered a hurricane. Two ships came to the rescue, but could only save a fraction of the passengers, so Captain Herndon chose to remain with his ship and passengers, and was lost with them.

But the example probably uppermost in Loxley's mind was that of Captain Edward Smith of the White Star Line's *Titanic*. On 15 April 1912 Captain Smith was in command of RMS *Titanic* when she struck an iceberg. Smith knew within minutes that the ship was doomed and did all in his power to prevent panic. He did not survive the sinking. There are conflicting accounts of his last minutes but the one the newspapers liked best had him locking himself in the ship's wheelhouse minutes before it went under. Robert Williams Daniel, a first class passenger who jumped from the stern immediately before the ship sank, told the *New York Herald* in its edition of 19 April 1912 how he had witnessed Captain Smith drown in the ship's wheelhouse. 'I saw Captain Smith on the bridge. My eyes seemingly clung to him. The deck from which I had leapt was immersed. The water had risen slowly, and was now to the floor of the bridge. Then it was to Captain Smith's waist. I saw him no more. He died a hero.'[12]

There are also conflicting accounts of Smith's last words. Reports said that, as the final plunge began, Smith shouted to his crew, 'Be British boys, be British!' and these words are engraved on his memorial. However, it is likely a myth made up by the press at the time, as not one member of the surviving crew claimed he said anything like this. One crew man said that, as water began to flood the bridge, Smith's last words were, 'Well boys, you've done your duty and done it well. I ask no more of you. I release you. You know the rule of the sea. It's every man for himself now, and God bless you.'[13] There are echoes in these valedictory phrases of those used by Loxley himself, 'Lads, this is the last, all hands for themselves, and may God bless you and guide you to safety.'

George Bernard Shaw was typically scathing. Writing a month after the loss of the *Titanic* he commented that the typical British shipwreck had three 'romantic demands' in particular: that the cry 'Women and children first' should be heard; that all men aboard ('except the foreigners') should be heroes, and the captain a superhero; and that 'everybody should face death without a tremor'.[14]

J. Bruce Ismay, the managing director of White Star Lines, escaped the wreck and was forever afterwards vilified for doing so, for breaking the 'rules' of expected gentlemanly behaviour. After the disaster Ismay was berated by both the American and the British press for deserting the ship while women and children were still on board. Some newspapers called him the 'Coward of the Titanic' or 'J. Brute Ismay' and suggested that the White Star flag be changed to a yellow liver. The writer Ben Hecht, a newspaperman in Chicago, wrote a coruscating poem which contrasted the actions of Captain Smith and Ismay. The final verse reads: 'To hold your place in the ghastly face of death on the sea at night is a seaman's job, but to flee with the mob, is an owner's noble right.'[15]

And so on January 1st 1915 Loxley knew well the expectations that he had to live up to. The examples of art, literature, the sports field, the soldiers and sailors off Danger Point and the *Titanic* were etched into his consciousness. He efficiently superintended the abandonment of the ship and then calmly awaited his fate.*** 'It was a second *Birkenhead*,' extolled the *Belfast Evening Telegraph*.[16]

***The tradition continues to this day. When Captain David Hart Dyke was commanding HMS *Coventry* in the Falklands campaign of 1982, his ship was attacked and sunk by Argentine planes. Hart Dyke was the last to leave his vessel and received severe burns for his pains.

13

Pro Patria

My friend, you would not tell with such high zest
To children ardent for some desperate glory,
The old Lie; Dulce et decorum est
Pro patria mori.

(Wilfred Owen, Dulce et Decorum est)

The fateful notifications of death were sent out to the next of
kin on 5 January. It was a typed standard letter, with blanks
where a clerk could enter the name of the deceased by hand.
Up and down the nation, parents, wives, brothers began to
receive the dread communication:

> I regret to inform you that HMS *Formidable* was sunk on the 1st
> instant and that the name_____, rating,
> _____official   number
> _____, who is believed to have been on
> board, does not appear in the list of survivors received in this
> department. In the circumstances it is feared that, in the absence
> of any evidence to the contrary, he must be regarded as having
> lost his life.

The tone was not exactly brimming over with empathy.

A major problem for the Admiralty was that they had only a
limited idea of who had been on board anyway. The official

file shows frantic telegrams to the hospital at Chatham, to the barracks and to other vessels attempting to locate ratings and place them as on board or not.

Midshipman Ivor Gregor MacGregor was surprised to see himself listed as dead when he was, in fact, very much alive and on another ship. An orphan from the age of 7, MacGregor had joined *Formidable* in July 1914 having been a cadet and then midshipman RNR since the year before. He had left the ship on 26 December to join, ironically, HMS *Diamond*.

Mrs Emma King wrote to the Admiralty from Rotherhithe having read of the death of her marine son in the *Daily Chronicle*; she enquired as to the truth of the report as she had received no official communication. It had been sent to the wrong address. The mother of Private R.A. Lawrence read in the papers that her son was alive and was showered with congratulations by friends and family. It turned out that he was dead, although her letter of enquiry seemed more concerned with ascertaining how much of his pay she would receive.

For those who had joined up from the Reserve the communication process was both complex and slow, for a letter was first sent to the RNR depot where they had joined up for onward transmission to the next of kin.

And so, slowly, the news of the death toll spread round the country and families everywhere sought solace in grief and grieving. Chatham honoured its dead with a memorial service in St George's Chapel, Royal Barracks, Chatham on January 8th. The large congregation included Loxley's widow Gladys and his orphaned son, as well as the mayors of Chatham and Gillingham and other civic dignitaries. For Gladys the service must have been doubly difficult for her father had died the day after her husband, aged 61.

And Thanatos had not finished with the Loxley family. The Reverend A.S. Loxley and his wife had five children, four boys and a daughter; only the girl and one son would survive the war. Noel Loxley's death made headline news; but his brothers also sacrificed their lives in the maw of the war to end all wars.

Vere Duncombe Loxley had been educated at Eton College, like his elder brother. He joined the Royal Marines Light Infantry and was 'Mentioned in Despatches' for his bravery during the evacuation from Gallipoli. In 1916 he held the rank of acting major when he was killed in action on November 13th during the great, and tragic, Somme offensive. He is buried in the Knightsbridge Cemetery, Mesnil-Martinsart.

Reginald Victor Byron Loxley, once of Radley College, joined the Royal Naval Air Service and flew over the Western Front, gaining the rank of acting captain. He died in Paris of his wounds on 18 Oct 1918, just 24 days before the war ended, aged 43, old for an airman.

The youngest boy, Gerald Herbert, 29 when war broke out and an alumnus of Malvern College and Oriel, Oxford, was also an airman, achieving the rank of major in the RAF and being awarded by the French the rank of *Chevalier, Légion d'honneur,* and the *Croix de guerre (avec palmes).* He married late, in 1930, and there were no children from the marriage. He and his sister Gladys Marjorie were the only survivors of this blighted family and neither produced male heirs. Only Noel Loxley had sired a son to further the family line, and he was aged just 9 when his father died.

The family's sacrifice is honoured at the little church of St Mary's Northchurch (near Berkhamsted), where the Reverend Loxley had once been curate. The family had lived locally for many years and Noel Loxley owned the manor of Norcott. On the occasion of the dedication of the village war memorial in March 1920, Edward, Prince of Wales (as Duke of Cornwall), the future Edward VIII, presented the church with a replacement white ensign, the Royal Navy's flag, in token of the Loxley family's loss. A stone tablet in the south transept, surrounded by various windows associated with the Duncombe and Loxley families, further commemorates their sacrifice (see also Appendix 4).

Captain Loxley is also remembered in the officer's mess at HMS *Excellent*, Portsmouth. A simple brass plaque for each officer who passed through the Gunnery School records their name, ship and date of death under the inscription *Dulce et decorum est Pro Patria Mori*. Situated on the half landing of the main stairs to the first floor, Loxley's name is on the upper row, next to his gunnery officer, Lieutenant Commander H.L. Street, who was also lost with the ship. There are also dedications to Loxley on the Lamport war memorial (the place of his birth) and on the Eastbourne roll of honour.

It might be noted *en passant* that the gods of war had not yet done with the Loxleys. Noel Loxley's son Peter, who gave up his pet dog to be a friend to his father, was educated at Eton and Trinity College Oxford, and later became a senior civil servant in the Foreign Office. He was killed in an aircraft accident on 1 February 1945 on his way to the Yalta Conference that was to divide up Europe for the next 60 years. Peter was at the time First Secretary and 'the star of the Foreign Office, widely tipped by his colleagues to one day succeed Sir Alex Cadogan as Permanent Under-Secretary'.[1] Aged only 39, he died when the Avro York in which he was travelling crashed into the sea off Lampedusa Island after a series of navigational errors. He too has his memorial in St Mary's church, a stained glass window in the south transept.

Bruce, Captain Loxley's Airedale terrier, has his own memorial at Abbotsbury, as previously noted. But he also achieved literary immortality in a book, *Captain Loxley's Little Dog*, published in 1915 by Hodder and Stoughton and the product of an anonymous author who also claimed authorship of *Where's Master?* It is a relentlessly twee tale of the sinking, told from the dog's perspective; a work of jingoism and propaganda to stir the hearts of (presumably) young boys throughout the empire. It includes Loxley telling Bruce to 'keep cool boy, keep cool, be British'.

Formidable was a Chatham ship (as was *Bulwark*). Their crews predominantly came from the Chatham base and barracks and all of the dead are commemorated on the great Chatham Naval War Memorial and on many local ones up and down the country. Such were the losses from these twin disasters that Chatham became known as 'the Town of Tears' after the loss of *Formidable*.[2] One street – Castle Street – in the town lost three men: Private Herbert Philips, RMLI, who left a wife and three children; Private Robert Kemp, also RMLI, and Able Seaman Albert Botley, just 19 years old. Chatham town gave up civilians too. The canteen on board *Formidable* was run by a contract caterer, Messrs R. Dickenson and Co. Their employees Canteen Manager Alfred P. Andrews and server Albert Corby went down with the ship.

Among those remembered on the Chatham Memorial was Stoker George Murphy, aged 42, who was Royal Naval Reserve, called up at the outbreak of war to expand *Formidable*'s nucleus crew. He left a wife and six children. Another stoker, Albert Brown, was only 21 when he died. His name appears on the Dover town war memorial as well. Able Seaman Daniel Cannon, 21, was one of nine Cannon family members who served in the war, six in the navy. He too appears on the Dover memorial. A son-in-law to the family, Thomas Kennett, was also serving aboard *Formidable* and he also died with the ship. Leading Stoker Charles Swaby, 27, is another whom Dover claims as its own. Albert Ellender, Dover born, a 29-year-old leading seaman, left a wife and little girl. In December 1915 they placed a poem in the local paper:

> We have lost you, we who loved you
> We like the others must be brave
> For we know that you are lying

In a British sailor's grave.
Friends may think that we forget him
When at times we are apt to smile
Little knowing what is hidden
Beneath the surface all the while.

G.W.H. 'Harry' Adams was an assistant clerk in the paymaster's office. His memorial belies his lowly status, for in St Mark's church, Portsmouth there is a stained glass window in the Lady Chapel dedicated to his memory. Dated 1915 it reads:

To the Glory of God
And in loving memory
Of GWH (Harry) Adams
Clerk RN of HMS
Formidable

Portsmouth also honours the memory of Ship's Steward's Assistant Reginald Alfred Laws who is listed on the Roll of Honour in St Wilfrid's church.

The parish of Northbourne, near Deal in Kent, lost two if its menfolk to *Formidable*, Seaman George Brading and Chief Petty Officer Walter Horton. Horton had joined the navy at 16 years old and but for the war was looking forward to retiring on a pension. He was married with two small children aged 18 months and 2 years 6 months, together with two step-children aged 5 and 8. His memorial is in St Augustine's church in the village. How his wife coped is not recorded. Leading Seaman E.A.L. Baber was buried at Portland. His mother was issued with a railway travel warrant by the Admiralty to allow her to attend.

Fleet Paymaster Percy J. Ling was one of the quintet of the most senior officers who went down with the ship. He left behind a wife of eleven years and a son aged 6. His duties would have included ensuring that the confidential books and codes on board were destroyed, which involved him staying in his cabin until his task was completed. He has the distinction, shared with Loxley and few others, of appearing on several memorials – Chatham, St Dunstans, Cranbrook, Kent, an interior cross of a briar rose design in stone, and Sissinghurst civic war memorial.

But *Formidable* also spread tragedy all over the country and some seamen have memorials further afield. Able Seaman Oliver Tidy, 20, came from the Surrey village of Ewhurst where his father was the local chimney sweep. He is remembered on the village war memorial at the church of St Peter and St Paul and on a plaque in the neighbouring settlement of Ellen's Green. The local newspaper reported that a memorial service for Oliver was held at the Congregational Church on January 15th.[3] Private Roland Walter Woods RMLI was 19 when he died. He had been a Post Office labourer in Wokingham until he joined up in 1912. He is remembered on the Binfield, Berks, war memorial and at Chatham. Midshipman Frank Bousfield Somerville was from Cumberland where his father was a commercial traveller in flour. He is commemorated on the Roll of Honour at his school, Trinity, Carlisle.

Many villages and towns were decimated by the Great War but the small parish of Caldecot, Cambs, lost only three men to the war; one of them was a 'Formidable', Stoker Victor Harrup. He is remembered on the Roll of Honour in the parish church of St Michael and on the Chatham monument.

Mechanician Harry Phipps came from Borrowash in Derbyshire. One of four children to Annie and Enoch (a railway guard) he followed his father into the railway as a fireman; but it was dull work and in 1900, aged 17, he joined the navy as a Stoker Second Class. The life suited him and he was regularly promoted, transferring to *Formidable* in 1911 and attaining the rank of mechanician, a promotion from the stoker branch and equivalent in rank to a petty officer. He was lost with the ship and, as a Chatham man, he too has his place on the Chatham memorial.

On the same day as the sinking the *Scarborough Mercury* headlined 'British Battleship Sunk – expected loss of 700 lives – fears for Scarborough men'. In fact the Yorkshire town gave three lives to *Formidable*'s watery grave. First Class Petty Officer Henry Purcell Jaques had joined the navy as a Boy Second Class aged 16 and worked his way up the ladder to the highest rank he could legitimately hope to hold in the service of that time. The son of a fish salesman's clerk, and 32 when he died, he is remembered on the Chatham memorial, at Dean Road Cemetery in Scarborough and on St Mary's church Roll of Honour in that town. Robert Smithson, Stoker First Class was 22 when the ship went down. Son of a bird dealer, woodworker and later milk dealer he is remembered at Chatham and also at Oliver's Mount war memorial in Scarborough. And 20-year-old Ordinary Seaman Charles Frederick Smith, whose father was a carver and guilder in Scarborough, had been an artist before joining up, a creative life snuffed out by the sea he loved to paint. He is commemorated on the Plymouth war memorial on the Hoe.

Yorkshire also lost Midshipman John Slingsby, aged just 16, son of the Reverend Slingsby, Rector of Kirby-Sigston and resident at Scriven Hall, Knaresborough, the ancestral home of the Slingsbys of Scriven since the fourteenth century. In 1916 Mrs Slingsby caused a memorial tablet to be placed in St Oswald's Church, Farnham (Yorks). Sculpted in marble it was surmounted by a Union Jack, under which was a model in relief of *Formidable* herself. On the tablet was inscribed:

In loving memory of Midshipman John Slingsby, born July 11th, 1898, youngest son of the Rev. Charles and Susan A. Slingsby. He lost his life on HMS Formidable, in the war against Germany, on the 1st January, 1915; also his great friend, Geoffrey Ernest Cadle, born March 17th, 1898. They both went through the rough sea

together to another land. Remember O Lord, the souls of the
faithful departed.
All that life contains of torture, toil and treason,
Shame, dishonour, death to them we're
but a name;
Here as boys they dwelt through all the
singing season,
And ere the day of sorry departed
as they came.

There were three men from Sheffield on the ship. Two were
lost, Ordinary Seaman Thomas Ball and Private Ernest Booth
RMLI, but Chief Petty Officer Richardson survived, rescued
by *Topaze*. Bradford gave up Private Frank Smithies, an
engineering fitter back home who had volunteered as a RMLI
private.

Stoker Alexander Chantrell, fished up from the sea near
Brixham, was buried in Stockton-on-Tees. His body had been
identified by his father Joseph, a naval reservist himself, who
had made the four-day, 660-mile return trip to claim him and
attended the inquest in his uniform. Alexander's family had
received a letter from him the day after the sinking, in which
he said that he was in 'good health and hoped to be getting
some leave soon'.[4] At the inquest a police sergeant gave
Chantrell senior a penny found in his son's uniform pocket,
and the jury donated their fees to the bereaved parent. Joseph
Chantrell commented 'that he was grateful for all that had
been done and broke down in tears when handed the
penny'.[5] Stoker Chantrell returned to his last resting place
in a coffin draped with a Union flag. He was not the only
victim from the north-east. The Roll of Honour published in
the *Darlington and Stockton Times* of 16 January contained
seven names of which four were lost with *Formidable*:
Alexander Chantrell, George Geldard and John Hillen of
Darlington, and Edward Jobling of Gosforth.

Thomas Laming was a sick berth attendant whose father

141

was a naval pensioner. He is remembered at All Saints church, South Wimbledon. Harry Nobes Beresford was a 49-year-old naval pensioner, recalled to the colours as Ship's Corporal; his memorial is in St Leonard's, Woolaton, Notts. Petty Officer Stoker William John Foad, son of an agricultural labourer, is on the Roll of Honour at St Mary's Chislet, Kent and Reculver war memorial. Stoker Jack French, of Thundersly, Essex, left a widow Annie, son John and daughter also Annie. And so the losses rolled across the country; Mechanician John Bygrave in Waterford, Herts; Seaman Alfred Cook in Great Oakley, Essex; Officer's Steward Robert Charles Noakes, RMLI, married with a wife living in Gillingham but remembered in Reddish, Cheshire.

Scotland too felt the cold breath of *Formidable*'s loss in Aberdeen born and educated hero Sub Lieutenant Herbert Shinnie, who had selflessly found floats for others, leaving none for himself. His father was a carriage and motor vehicle manufacturer in the granite city and owned the Albion Motors concession for the region. It would be a long trip to see his son's name on the Chatham memorial. Surgeon William Mellis Mearns had qualified in medicine at Aberdeen University. The official record of his death states, 'On 1 January 1915 this ship was torpedoed when going down Channel, and unfortunately this most promising officer lost his life. His reports show that he was an officer of high attainments.' Another of the surgeons lost, 28-year-old Septimus Hibbert, who had joined up on the outbreak of war from his post as house surgeon at St George's Hospital, London, is remembered on the war memorial at Compton and Shawford, Hampshire, high up on Shawford Down.

Not all of the dead of Lyme Regis are buried and honoured there. Two of them were the twins, John and Henri Villiers Russell, both sick berth attendants. They had both had been employed at the locomotive works in Crewe, in the joinery shop; John, a talented artist, had received offers of work elsewhere but refused them to stay with his brother and widowed mother. Together they jointly ran the local Primitive Methodist Sunday school and were members of the St. John's ambulance brigade and the Royal Navy Sick Berth Reserve in which capacity, during the works' annual holiday of July 1914, they joined *Formidable* as sick berth attendants for training purposes. They never returned home. Their grieving mother claimed their bodies and, with financial support from the superintendent of the works, took them to their home town of Crewe where, as has been described, they were buried in St. Michael's Churchyard, Coppenhall. An Italian marble headstone, inscribed 'Fast they stood' and 'For Right and Good', marks the spot. They are also commemorated in a street name (Villiers Russell Close) on the quondam site of the Methodist church where they had worshipped and by a plaque in Crewe's municipal building. It reads in part, 'This memorial is dedicated to Henri and John Russell who served and died together in battle on the same ship. This incident started a debate in the Houses of Parliament to change the Naval Law that no brothers should be made to serve (unless they wish to do) on the same Naval Vessel. This law is still being enforced.' Amazingly they were not the only sick berth attendants from Crewe to die as a result of the sinking. Senior Reserve Sick Berth Attendants Albert E. Kinlay, who died on his 23rd birthday, and John Burnell were also Crewe men and yet another, Tom Hassall, had died when *Formidable*'s sister ship the *Bulwark* blew up the previous November.

Leading Seaman John Pells, who died as the boat reached the Lyme Regis shore, was also taken by his parents and buried in his local cemetery at King's Lynn. Boy First Class Bernard Smyth is buried in Lyme but has his memorial at Holy Trinity, Cuckfield, a brass plaque on the south wall of the nave, engraved 'sometime choirboy of Ansty who gave his life for his country in the loss of HMS Formidable Jan 1 1915, aged 17'. Signal Boy Frederick Norman, whose body was washed ashore at Charmouth a month after the sinking, was taken back to his place of birth and is buried in March cemetery, Cambridgeshire. His grave was white marble with four corner posts.

The loss of his son-in-law, Commander Charles Ballard, was a blow to Admiral Burney who had just gone up to Scapa Flow to command the First Battle Squadron of the Grand Fleet. Rear-Admiral Alexander Duff, of the Fourth Battle Squadron, saw him on 8 January and noted in his diary that 'he is naturally terribly depressed'.[6] Ballard has his memorial in the church of Saints Peter and Paul, Aston Rowant, Oxon, where his father, mother and siblings are all buried. It reads:

> Ad Dei Gloriana
> In loving memory of Charles Frederick Ballard, Commander Royal Navy, 2nd son of Lt. Col. JF Ballard who, with 548 other officers and men, lost his life in the sinking of HMS Formidable which was torpedoed by a German submarine in the English Channel Jan 1 1915
> This tablet is erected by his widow Violet Hazel

It is a simple bronze plaque set into the wall. His name is also recorded on the wooden war memorial in the church, put in place as late as 1956. He was one of ten men from the village who gave their lives.

Lieutenant Trevor H.S. Tatham, 27 years old, went down with the ship, but his mother Frances, whose husband had died the previous November, already knew of his death. Awakened by the bells ringing in the New Year, she saw her son standing at the end of her bed and knew instantly he would not be returning to her.[7] Tatham had joined the navy aged 14 and had attained the rank of torpedo officer by 1914. He had clearly been destined for a bright future. Unusually intelligent (he had taken five firsts in his various navy exams), he received glowing write ups on his navy 'report card'. 'Clever and Capable'; 'judgement beyond his years'; and from that stern judge of young officers, William Pakenham, 'very promising and industrious'. *Formidable* had been his first ship ten years previously as a midshipman. His name is on the Roll of Honour at Amesbury School in Surrey.

Another officer to lose his life was Lieutenant Hugh C.H. Coxe, aged 26, of Shefford Woodlands, Berks. This was tragedy enough for his family, but his two brothers Arthur and Clifford were to lose their lives on the Western Front aged only 18 and 19. All three are remembered in St Stephen's church by the windows, ceramic plaque and pew carvings that honour all eleven men of the village who died in the war.

Nine masons went down with the ship. According to the 1921 Masonic Roll of Honour, 3,225 masons of all ranks and services died in the Great War. They are commemorated by the Masonic Peace Memorial (later Freemasons Hall), Great Queen Street, completed in 1933. Chatham alone had nine lodges, so it may be assumed that freemasonry was relatively popular in the navy; indeed Churchill was a mason, although he never achieved a high masonic rank, as was Loxley's brother Vere (Navy Lodge, Province of London).

France too holds some of *Formidable*'s diaspora and memory. Able Seaman George Ashbee's body was carried by the tides to the French coast and is buried at Janval Cemetery, Dieppe.

The sinking of the *Formidable* spread its tentacles of loss even across the Atlantic. Canada gave men to the tragedy. Captain John Deed RMLI, 38 years old and born in St Albans, had settled in Fernie, British Columbia, and had come over with the first contingent of Canadian soldiers to volunteer before transferring to the Marines. His father was vicar of St Nicolas parish church in Nuneaton and Deed is commemorated there. There were two men from Ontario on board.

145

Yeoman of Signals Fred Ames was rescued by *Topaze* but Marine Corporal C.W. West was drowned. Lieutenant-Commander Street's death left a wife who hailed from Halifax, Nova Scotia.

Rich and poor, landed and landless, young and old, *Formidable* did not discriminate in death. And she was not alone. Altogether, in the month of January 1915, the navy lost over 1,000 men.

Nor did her nemesis survive the war. Kapitänleutnant Rudolf Schneider became one of Germany's most successful U-boat commanders, sinking 140,783 tons of Allied shipping. He also became one of the most notorious, following his sinking of the passenger ship SS *Arabic* on 19 August 1915, 50 miles south of Kinsale. The White Star Line ship lost 44 passengers and crew, including three Americans. Following on from the sinking of the *Lusitania*, the torpedoing of the *Arabic* further angered US President Wilson and inflamed American public opinion. It had two results. First, Kaiser Wilhelm and his chancellor, Bethmann, ordered further limitations on the use of the submarine weapon which rendered it largely useless; second, it made the case easier for America to enter the war after Germany resumed unrestricted submarine warfare in 1917. But Schneider too was to become one of the fallen. On 13 October 1917, while in command of U-87, he was washed overboard during a storm in the North Sea. He was rescued and brought back aboard the submarine unconscious, but died shortly afterwards and was buried at sea. He was one of the Kaiser's top twenty submariners in terms of tonnage sunk. Neither did U-87 survive long, being sunk with all hands three months later.

During the period 4 August 1914 to 11 November 1918 the Royal Navy lost a total of 43,244 men dead; of these 34,654 were navy and 8,590 Royal Naval Division – i.e., killed fighting as infantry or artillery. A further 5,158 navy personnel were injured while the Royal Naval Division men suffered

20,165 injured, a reflection of their exposure on the Western and other fronts. Outside the navy, a further 15,313 men were killed serving in the merchant marine or fishing fleet. All told, therefore, some 83,880 were killed or wounded in the king's cause and wearing royal or merchant marine colours.[8]

This is a large number by any standard. It is more than a capacity crowd at Old Trafford football stadium (75,731) or Soldier Field, Chicago (61,500). But in the context of the British military losses in the First World War, it pales into insignificance. Over one million British and Commonwealth soldiers died in that conflict and a further two million were wounded (and one million returned home disabled). Some 17% of officers and 12% of ordinary soldiers who served were killed (for the navy the comparable figures were 5.3% and 7.3%). Total losses on all sides were just under 10 million with 20 million wounded.

As a consequence it is easy to overlook the sacrifice made at sea; it seems almost trivial compared to the mega-death inflicted on land. The focus at Remembrance Day services and in populist books and films is on the trenches, the army, the mass slaughter in France and Belgium. But this is to overlook the point that every death was an individual, a family sundered, a wife left on her own, a child now father-less. The loss felt by the bereaved of *Formidable* was no less painful than that of the families of any soldier killed in the mud and slime of the land war. The sacrifice of Loxley and Ballard, the courage of Carroll and Bing, the selfless rescue by Pillar should all rank just as high in the pantheon of memory as the heroes of the trenches.

Lest we forget, lest we forget.

14

Patriotism and Propaganda

It is said that the Germans ascribe their defeat and downfall largely to the effects of propaganda – mainly British – on their population and armies and that in the eyes of their High Command Lord Northcliffe himself was a general no less to be feared and respected than Foch himself.

(article in *Naval Review*, May 1919)

The sinking of HMS *Formidable* made headlines in all the newspapers. But they did not dwell on the shocking deaths involved; instead the stories focused on the courage and bearing of the crew. Patriotism was at the fore, the stoic, self-sacrificing, ironically humorous, beau-ideal of Britishness was the main story. *The Times* led the way on January 4th with a piece entitled 'The Captain and his Commander'. It majored on Loxley's calmness, the assurance with which he and Ballard tried to get the boats away, the appeal to 'be British boys'. Loxley was depicted as *Homo newboltiensis*, the insouciant school captain marshalling his team, the brave self-sacrificing officer with his loyal second and his dog, awaiting the end with courage and dignity.

The story went round the world. The *New York Tribune* put the story on its front page on January 2nd. 'Battleship Formidable sunk by a submarine in Channel. 600 men perish,

150 saved' it screamed. The *Springfield Republican* of the same day had 'Battleship Formidable sunk. Goes to the bottom, 600 of crew perish', while the *Boston Evening Globe* (late edition) had 'British Battleship Formidable sunk. 700 sent to bottom by mine or submarine'.

But other newspapers made much of the bravery and phlegm of the rescued sailors. Their fame reached all corners of the empire; newspapers in Australia and New Zealand for example, covered their stories in patriotic tones. The qualities of Britishness were much trumpeted. One newspaper has a survivor describing Captain Loxley as a 'real true Britisher'.[1] The same publication has another sailor describe the matelot who stuffed his trousers into a hole in the boat as 'a Briton', to which the matelot replied, 'Oh, we don't take notice of such things.' Back at home the *Daily Graphic* (the first British daily illustrated newspaper) of January 4th featured a photograph of the men rescued by the *Provident* with their saviours under the headline 'Seventy rescued by five', and the next day the editor put these Brixham survivors on the front page with a picture of them boarding the train to go home. The *Bridport News* of January 8th headlined '199 saved' and 'thrilling narratives'.

The hagiolatry of Captain Loxley was a common feature in newspaper reports. For example, 'Captain Loxley combined a loveable personality with that business manner which has become a tradition among captains in the navy. The crew worshipped him as a man who would hold impromptu lectures on the war and in every other way seek to get to their hearts.'[2] In an attempt to portray Loxley's human side and his generous, true British character the authorities released the transcript of a letter that he had recently sent to his old Nanny, together with a Christmas gift. It demonstrates the quotidian life that pertained prior to the sinking:

My Dear Old Nan

My very best love and best wishes to you for Christmas and the New Year, and may we soon beat the Germans. We are having a quiet time, but you never know when anything may happen.

Peter has gone to school and is home for his first holidays ... he was much braver going to school than I.

Everyone seems well at Gloucester [where his mother lived] but I have only seen mother once for about ten minutes during the last two years

With love
Yours lovingly

Noel Loxley[3]

Mounted and titled memorial photographs and postcards of the ship were produced for sale with Loxley's portrait inset in the corner. *The Sphere* ('the Empire's Illustrated Weekly') in its January 23rd issue carried a picture of Loxley and Bruce in an arched-framed memorial article.

The bravery and stoicism of the crew was extolled throughout the land. The *Belfast Evening Telegraph* of January 9th ran a feature around Seaman Gunner Hughes (of Banbridge, Co Down) who was depicted as wanting to pay off 'old scores' with the Germans. 'Notwithstanding his nerve-trying experience and long exposure to the cold he looks the perfection of physical fitness. One cannot get in touch with such men without being impressed with the fighting spirit of the Navy, which, however many *Formidables* may go to the bottom, is ever-living and indestructible.' The reporter continued by asking Hughes, 'I suppose the Navy wish that the Germans would come out into the open so we could have a straightforward scrap with them ... the only answer was a knowing smile that was more significant than language.'

The same newspaper, commenting on the survival of local

man Stoker Connor in its January 26th issue, noted that 'their endurance is a lasting tribute to the British sailor and it speaks highly of the courage of Connor to state that but for shock caused by the cold and exposure and a tendency to rheumatic pain he has almost recovered from the experience'. Connor, who was still being treated by a doctor in Belfast, might of course have held a different view.

The *Sydney Morning Herald* of February 12th tipped its hat to Newbolt with its story headlined 'a brave captain' and 'everybody played the game', while the *Daily Mail* waxed lyrical, stating 'in the years of our sea supremacy we have grown accustomed to heroic naval deeds but few more glorious tales can ever have been related than that of the loss of HMS *Formidable*'.[4] This, it should be remembered, for a ship that sank by undetected torpedo attack with the loss of nearly 600 men.

Poems were written to celebrate the event. The paean to Marine Stanley Reed, which featured in many newspapers, has already been noted in Chapter 7. Another, by one F. Wood, 'The Loss of the Formidable on New Year's Morn' gained similar coverage. Written in iambic tetrameter, it begins 'The New Years's morn had but awoke, when on our ears great sorrow broke', and continues for over 100 lines of prosody that would make McGonagall blush. Of Loxley, the poet waxes:

> Their Captain, stalwart and so true,
> At his post when the last blast blew
> May they be piloted to that shore
> Where there is peace for evermore.[5]

Another poet (anonymous) offered 'Brave souls of the Formidable', with the last verse:

> Brave souls of the Formidable
> At home, your loss, our sorrow,

151

Sacrificed for right and good
And England's tomorrow.[6]

William Pillar was lionised in both local and national press and rewarded by a grateful nation, as described in Chapter 7. He and his crew also featured in a newsreel by Gaumont News, resplendent in oversized flat hats, and his fishing smack was made the subject of a jigsaw, a painting and countless photo prints.

The ship's badge presented by the survivors of Lyme Regis was framed by the townsfolk before being hung in the Guild Hall. The legend describes that the emblem of an Eagle standing on a crown was originally Lord Rodney's crest, summoning the memory of the famous Admiral Sir George Brydges Rodney who defeated the French in 1782 at the Battle of the Saintes, ending French naval prestige in Caribbean waters and removing the threat to Jamaica. A previous *Formidable* had been his flagship. Admiral Rodney's descendent had, at the launching of the later *Formidable*, been asked if the ship could use his armorial, to which he replied that 'it would be an honour'. The plaque describes how 'this honour was kept untarnished by the last signal of Captain Loxley before the ship went down and kept undimmed by the conduct of each one lost in the Formidable'.[7]

Politicians too were 'on message'. The Liberal leader in the Lords, Earl Crewe (Robert Crewe-Milnes) gave a speech to the House in which he eulogised the courage of Loxley and his men. 'I should like to tell the House that after the ship was struck her Captain signalled to another ship that she was not to stand by because he believed that there was a submarine in the neighbourhood.' Crewe went on to emphasise the equalities of self-sacrifice and stoicism so prized in the propaganda of the time: 'In that he acted in a manner worthy of the highest traditions of the British navy and I am sure it will be a consolation to those whose relatives lost their lives to know that they went down with their last thoughts for their comrades in the fleet.' Just how much of a consolation he expected it to be was not noted.[8]

And, of course, even the dogs were feted, Loxley's Bruce being the hero of the book *Captain Loxley's Little Dog'* (where Loxley is depicted as saying to him 'keep cool boy, keep cool, be British', an echo of the alleged last words of Captain Smith of the Titanic). Bruce's breed was flexible according to region. In the *Belfast Evening Telegraph* he became an 'Irish Terrier'. Lassie, apart from her outing to Crufts, gave a dog-loving public hours of amusement through reading of her exploits in newspapers and seeing them on the newsreel.[9]

But what was the reason for this outpouring of film, prose and verse? And was it spontaneous or orchestrated? The British public were, at this time, still relatively unaware of the growing slaughter on the Western Front, largely as the result of successful government censorship, although the growing weight of 'I regret to inform you' telegrams was making it more and more difficult to conceal. As an example, 300,000 French soldiers had been killed or wounded in the first three weeks of the 'Battle of the Frontiers', August 1914 (27,000 met their end on the 22nd alone), but no indication whatsoever of this toll appeared in any British newspaper.

The vehicle which allowed the home government to contain the news was DORA – the Defence of the Realm Act of 1914. DORA ushered in a variety of authoritarian social control mechanisms, such as censorship: viz 'No person shall by word of mouth or in writing spread reports likely to cause disaffection or alarm among any of His Majesty's forces or among the civilian population.'[10] Passed by the House of Commons on August 8th, without any debate, the law was designed to help prevent invasion and to keep morale at home high. The legislation gave the government executive powers to suppress published criticism, imprison without trial and to commandeer economic resources for the war effort. DORA imposed censorship of journalism and of letters coming home from the front line. The press was subject to controls on reporting troop movements, numbers or any other operational information that could be exploited by the enemy. People who breached the regulations with intent to assist the enemy could be sentenced to death.

In August 1914 the government had established the War Office Press Bureau under F. E. Smith (later Lord Birkenhead). The idea was this organisation would censor news and telegraphic reports from the British army and then issue it to the press. War Minister Lord Kitchener decided to appoint Colonel Ernest Swinton to become the British army's official journalist on the Western Front and the only person allowed to submit reports from the front back to Britain. Swinton's reports were first censored at G.H.Q. in France and then personally vetted by Kitchener before being released to the press. Letters written by members of the armed forces to their friends and families were also read and censored by the military authorities. Additionally, only two photographers, both army officers, were allowed to take pictures of the battlefields. The penalty for anyone else caught taking a photograph of the war was death by firing squad.

As a consequence the general public remained largely unaware of the dreadful reverses borne by the French and the almost total destruction of the BEF – the British Expeditionary Force. The impression was maintained of a war of good versus evil, where noble British courage, chivalry and fair play was pitted against baby-killing, nun-raping, culture-destroying Germany. Reporting majored on individual acts of bravery and selflessness, the patriotic fervour of the troops, largely imaginary battlefield gains and the odd naval success such as the Battle of Heligoland Bight. It is against that context that the style of laudatory reporting of the *Formidable* disaster may be judged. (This public ignorance was not unique to Britain; French casualties after five months of war were 300,000 killed and 600,000 wounded. The figures were not made public at all – even at the war's end – and remained a secret throughout, experienced only at family or *commune* level. Some historians believe that this ignorance was what kept the French people in the war.)

At the outbreak of war, Britain did not have a propaganda machine as such, but it swiftly became obvious that Germany did. As a consequence, Lloyd George, the Chancellor of the Exchequer, was given the task of setting up a British War Propaganda Bureau (BWPB). Lloyd George appointed the writer, journalist and fellow Liberal MP, Charles Masterman – whom Beatrice Webb, in her diaries, was to note had an 'almost unnaturally close friendship'[11] with Churchill – to head the organisation. The headquarters were set up at Wellington House, the London headquarters of the National Insurance Commission, of which Masterman had been the chairman.

They began work at the beginning of September and swiftly recruited a stable of writers which included some of the best names of the day: William Archer, Arthur Conan Doyle, Arnold Bennett, John Masefield, Ford Madox Ford, G.K. Chesterton, Henry Newbolt, John Galsworthy, Thomas Hardy, Rudyard Kipling, Gilbert Parker, G.M. Trevelyan and H.G. Wells. In all fifty-two authors were recruited to the cause and they published a manifesto, signed by all of them, declaring it to be Britain's 'destiny of duty to uphold the rule of common justice between civilised peoples, to defend the rights of small nations and to maintain the free and law-abiding ideals of Western Europe against the rule of "Blood and Iron".' They were soon into their stride, Chesterton producing *The Barbarians of Berlin* in which he argued that England was fighting for the 'Long Arm of Honour', while Arnold Bennett, who with Wells was to be a prolific press polemicist in the Allied cause, penned *Liberty; a Statement of the British Cause.*

Masterman also engaged a tame stable of publishers, prominent among which were Hodder and Stoughton, who were to publish *Captain Loxley's Little Dog* and *Where's Master?* as a part of the domestic propaganda effort aimed at maintaining morale and moral tone on the Home Front. In all the BWPB was to publish almost 1,200 pamphlets and books during the course of the war.

Another author recruited by Masterman to the propaganda cause was the Scot, John Buchan. Buchan wrote two 'thrillers' in which his hero Richard Hannay pitted himself against the forces of darkness. In *The Thirty-Nine Steps*, published in August 1915 as a serial in *Blackwood's Magazine* and in October as a book, Buchan holds up Hannay as an example to his readers of an ordinary man who puts his country's interests before his own safety and is able to break a mysterious German spy ring, thus keeping his country's secrets safe. The story was a great success, especially with the men in the trenches. In *Greenmantle*, published by Hodder and Stoughton (Masterman's 'go to' publisher for propaganda) in 1916, Hannay is called in to investigate rumours of an uprising in the Muslim world and undertakes a perilous journey through enemy territory to meet his friend Sandy in Constantinople. Once there, he and his friends must thwart the Germans' plans to use religion to help them win the war, climaxing at the Battle of Erzurum. Buchan saw *Greenmantle* as an overtly jingoistic book, with the German characters portrayed as negative stereotypes and the British as the virtues personified. Among the book's fans were Baden-Powell and the Russian royal family.

Composers too were pressed into the effort. Edward Elgar, Britain's greatest composer, was the sound of the Edwardian empire and personified the 'bluff Englishman' (although actually a rather sensitive soul). When war broke out Elgar was horrified at the prospect of the carnage, but his patriotic feelings were nonetheless aroused and he composed *A Song for Soldiers*. He signed up as a special constable in the local police and later joined the Hampstead Volunteer Reserve. After the rape of Belgium by the invading Germans, Elgar wrote *Carillon* at the end of 1914, a recitation for speaker and orchestra in honour of 'poor little' Belgium and with words by the Belgian poet Emile Cammaerts ('Sing Belgians, Sing/Although our wounds may bleed'). The following year he produced *Polonia*, an orchestral piece in honour of Poland which utilised the Polish National Anthem and folk tunes. *Land of Hope and Glory* (originally written as 'Pomp and Circumstance March no.1' in 1901), already popular, became Britain's unofficial anthem, and his 1897 piece *The Banner of St George* gained renewed popularity. Also in 1915 Elgar set the poems of the war poet Laurence Binyon to music in *The Spirit of England* and, with Rudyard Kipling as librettist, produced in 1917 the popular *Fringes of the Fleet* in praise of the navy, which Elgar dedicated to 'my friend Admiral Lord Charles Beresford'.

The visual arts were also enjoined in the cause and some specifically celebrated the *Formidable*. *Provident*'s rescue of the men in the pinnace was immortalised by an unknown artist of the 'British School', while C.M. Padday produced the etching 'Captain Loxley giving his Last Order as the "Formidable" went down' for the *Illustrated London News*. One of the foremost British marine artists of the time, Charles John de Lacy, painted the watercolour 'HMS Formidable in distress', showing her last moments afloat and the brave tars on deck.

The British film industry was also suborned into the propaganda effort, making such films as *From Flower Girl to Red Cross Nurse* (1915) where a girl is rescued from suicide and becomes a nurse, and *Under the German Yoke*, also 1915, set in occupied France where a mayor's daughter shoots a Prussian captain and her old nurse brings the British army to save her father from execution. In the same year *How*

Lieutenant Rose RN spiked the enemy's guns depicts the eponymous hero signalling his flagship from land to destroy the German headquarters in a chateau.

Children's patriotic education was not neglected. Sir Edward Parrot wrote *The Children's Story of the War*. In the 1916 edition he lauded the behaviour of the sailors left on board *Formidable* after all the ship's boats had departed and the ship began to go under: 'On one part of the ship where the men could see there was no hope, all eyes were turned upward to the flagstaff, and then the Old Jack was saluted for the last time. The last impression of the scene left on my mind was a long line of saluting figures disappearing below the sky-line.'[12] A dutiful role model for the young and impressionable.

Even babies were recruited to the propaganda cause. In May 1915, nine months after the first of Kitchener's volunteers had departed for Flanders, thousands of illegitimate babies were born. Normally this would have been the signal for an outpouring of indignation concerning declining moral standards. However, these unfortunate infants were hastily dubbed 'war babies' by the patriotic press, and were soon regarded by Fleet Street, and even in official circles, as a contribution to replacing the manpower now being lost in the threshing machine of the Western Front.

Thus, although *Formidable* was a disaster in human terms, and no movie resulted from the story, it was possible to make it into a propaganda triumph of British pluck – and that is exactly what happened (see also Appendix 5). Loxley, Ballard, the survivors and the dogs all became tropes of national stoicism and bravery, fitting within an overall picture of British courage and sacrifice and obscuring the reality of the terror of a suffocating death at sea or maiming and mayhem on the Western Front.

Despite lying at the bottom of the sea, the old girl was still able to play her part in the war effort.

15

The Dogs of War

Cry Havoc and let slip the dogs of war.
(William Shakespeare, *Julius Caesar*)

Lassie the Collie and Bruce the Airedale had their moments of fame in 1915 and beyond. Immortalised in books, newsreels and newspapers their canine courage, intuition and loyalty inspired a dog-loving nation. They stood as symbols of British-ness and raised morale. But behind the scenes there were many dogs whose story would never be told and yet would undertake more practical tasks than the simple raising of the public's mood. An estimated 20,000 dogs served on the front line, particularly on the Western Front[1] and around 7,500 of them were killed in action.

As a result of policy or neglect, the British did not have trained army dogs (other than guard dogs) or any intention to deploy them. The Germans, on the other hand, had a force (*Sanitätshunde*) of 'mercy' dogs, trained to find the wounded and dying on the battlefield and carrying medical supplies, and had used them since the early 1800s.

At the outbreak of war there were no military dogs of any sort attached to the British army save for one sole Airedale, who served with the 2nd Battalion Norfolk Regiment as a sentry and accompanied the battalion to France, where he was eventually killed by a shell at the Battle of the Aisne. However, one Lt Col. Edwin Hautenville Richardson, a dog trial judge and aficionado in his spare time, was convinced of the essential role dogs could fill in wartime. Before the war he had been a frequent visitor to the continent and had seen the uses to which German and Russian military and police forces put their dogs. Now he built up a large kennel of dogs that underwent experimental training for sentry and patrol work.

Richardson began to supply dogs for such general work and found that Airedale Terriers displayed the best combination of qualities (and sent some to the Belgian army too, on request). In response to a letter from an officer in the Royal Artillery during the winter of 1916, Richardson turned his attention to training dogs specifically as messengers. His correspondent had pointed out that trained dogs would be able to keep up communication between an outpost and the battery during a heavy bombardment, when noise and communication difficulties rendered telephones practically useless and when the risk to human runners was enormous. On the first day of Neuve Chapelle in 1915, for example, it took nine hours for front line officers to get a message back to their corps commander and receive a reply. After some experimentation, Richardson successfully trained two Airedales to carry messages for two miles without problems and at the end of the year he was able to despatch two dogs, named Wolf and Prince, to France.

By now, among the massacre in the trenches, communication was becoming a major military problem. Telephone wires were blown up almost as quickly as they were laid down, radio was unreliable and difficult to use in war conditions and messengers – runners as they were known – were hugely vulnerable as they scampered up and down and over the trenches, and were specifically targeted by enemy snipers. Dogs suddenly seemed like an obvious answer. Faster, smaller and more agile than a human runner they could travel over any terrain – and were expendable too. Richardson's work, previously viewed as eccentric, now came into its own.

He was empowered to establish a War Dog Training School (at Shoeburyness in Essex). By way of a test, a graduate from this school travelled over 4,000 yards on the Western Front with a message to a brigade's headquarters. The dog travelled this distance, through very difficult terrain, in less than sixty minutes and beat all other methods tried.

Proof of success having been obtained, official sanction was given and a Major Waley MC RE was appointed supervisor of all dog operations in the field, once the dogs arrived in France. The main kennels were at Etaples (the main army base behind the lines) and placed under the command of the Royal Engineers Signal Corps who took responsibility in early 1917, with sectional kennels not far behind the front line. Each sectional kennel had a sergeant-in-charge, about 16 handlers and 48 dogs. The animals were then handed over to specially designated individuals in the front line battalions. Great care went into selecting the correct 'handler'. It was found that the best were men who had been gamekeepers, shepherds or hunt servants, although Richardson pointed out that the most important qualities were 'to be of an honest, conscientious character, with sympathetic understanding for animals ... using his own initiative to a great extent in handling his dogs ... men of intelligence and faithfulness to duty are absolutely essential.'[2]

As for the dogs, Airedales and collies were found to be excellently suited to messenger tasking, with lurchers and retrievers also prized. Surprisingly 'summer dogs' were also much used – so named because 'some are this and some are that'; mongrels, in other words. The messages went in tins slung around the dog's neck and the dogs were identified by a scarlet tally or collar. It was a military offence to stop a dog in its line of duty.

There were numerous tales of Airedales delivering their messages despite terrible injury and another Airedale hero soon emerged to line up alongside Bruce. One named Jack ran through half a mile of enemy fire to deliver his message. He arrived at headquarters with his jaw broken and one leg badly splintered, and directly after he had delivered the message he dropped dead in front of its recipient.[3]

Demand for dogs at the front soon outstripped the existing source of supply – Battersea Dogs' Home and the dogs' homes in other major cities of the UK – and the general public were asked to forsake their pets for the war effort. Given the nation's reputation as one of dog lovers, there was a surprisingly good response – although this might in part have been due to the introduction of food rationing, which made feeding pets more difficult. Some sent letters with their pets. One little girl wrote, 'We have let Daddy go to fight the Kaiser, and now we are sending Jack to do his bit.' Another letter was from a lady who noted, 'I have given my husband and my sons, and now that he too is required, I give my dog.'[4]

The demand was such that Richardson (and his wife who worked alongside him) were ordered to move their operation to Lyndhurst in Hampshire (and he moved again in 1919 to Bulford on Salisbury Plain). The messenger dog had proved its worth.

Note should also be made of the other roles played by dogs in the war. There were guard dogs, sentry dogs, scout dogs (to detect an approaching enemy), and not least there were companion dogs, sharing the privations of the trenches, cheering up the soldiery and often earning their keep by catching and killing the teeming rats. This was not confined to the army. Many dogs went to sea on Royal Navy ships and some suffered Bruce's fate. Brave Kit Cradock for example, Rear Admiral Sir Christopher Cradock, who died with his men at the Battle of Coronel on November 1st 1914, had his fox terrier with him for his final fatal mission.

At the end of the war Field Marshal Haig acknowledged the contribution that dogs had made to the war effort in one of his final despatches. And Richardson had no doubts at all that his charges had done their duty admirably. He wrote, 'The trained dog considers himself highly honoured by his position as a servant of His Majesty, and renders no reluctant service. From my observation along this line I have, in fact, come to the conclusion that a dog trained to some definite work, is happier than the average loafing dog, no matter how kindly the latter may be treated. I certainly found it to be the case with the army dogs.'[5] In this he might just have revealed himself as less perceptive than he thought!

So Lassie and Bruce represented just the tip of the iceberg. Honoured and lauded, they played their part in the propaganda war while their peers played theirs in the mud and stench of Flanders.

Part III

Wraiths

Beware lest you lose the substance by grasping at the shadow.
(Aesop, *The Dog and the Shadow*)

16

Memorials to the Fallen

When the public sets a war memorial up
Do those who really sweated get the credit?
No, some general wangles the prestige.
(Euripides, *Andromache*)

The names of the dead of *Formidable* are seen on war memorials across the land. Nearly every village and town has a memorial, sometimes elaborate, sometimes achingly simple (although there were 52 'thankful villages' that lost no menfolk to the war). Plaques in churches, Rolls of Honour, brass plates on walls, tall crosses, complex carvings; all sorts of design (and designers) were pressed into service to remember the dead. Britain had no history of such memorials before the First World War. A very occasional Boer War remembrance, stained glass or wall tablets in churches dedicated to the sons of the local squire or nobility; but no mass memorials. Why?

Prior to 1914, Britain's army had been small, professional and volunteer based. The ranks were often a haven for petty crooks, men of violence, the illiterate or uneducated, the unemployable, the detritus of society. As Wellington said of his men, 'I don't know what effect these men will have on the enemy, but by God, they terrify me.'[1] When they died on some far-flung field, they were perhaps not much missed. But 1914–18 was different. Britain's military was a first of all a volunteer army. Nearly 2.5 million men had enlisted before conscription was introduced in 1916 and the rate of volunteering was higher among the professional and white collar strata of society than among the 'working class'. These men were butchers, bakers and candlestick makers. They were teachers and tradesmen, professors and poets. They were loved sons, fathers and husbands. And they were deeply missed.

In total, 5.7 million British and Irish men served in the forces, of whom 723,000 were killed (6% of the male population aged 15–49). The middle and upper classes suffered in a way they had not done since the Middle Ages.* Approximately 12% of all the British soldiers who served were killed. But for peers, or sons of peers, the figure was 19%. Of all the men who graduated from Oxford in 1913, 31% were killed. Prime Minister Asquith lost his son; so did German chancellor Bethmann-Hollweg. Future Prime Minister Bonar-Law lost two sons, as did newspaper baron Viscount Rothermere. The cream of Britain's youth was cruelly washed away on a tide of blood.

The movement for remembrance probably started with the National Peace Day Celebration and the Peace Parade held in London on 19 July 1919. A cenotaph (from the Greek words *kenos* meaning 'empty' and *taphos* meaning 'tomb') of wood and plaster was designed by Sir Edwin Lutyens and erected in Whitehall as a temporary place of homage for the march past.

---

*Indeed in 1917–18 there arose growing middle class anger about how some industrial workers – who were exempt from conscription and regularly went on strike – were profiting from wartime wage increases while the middle class paid the 'blood tax' at the front.

Following the parade, members of the public placed flowers there and the structure quickly became a focal point of national grief for all those who had lost loved ones in the war.

Such was the need for a focus for public anguish that it was decided to erect a permanent memorial on the same site. Lutyens was again commissioned. His solemn and dignified design was built in Portland stone and finished in time for a parade to pass by it on 11 November 1920, to mark the interment of the British 'Unknown Warrior' at Westminster Abbey. Within a week 1.25 million people had passed by it and the base was ten feet deep in flowers. The Cenotaph was again the focus of a ceremony of remembrance on the anniversary of the Armistice on 11 November 1921 and subsequently became the location for the United Kingdom's national annual ceremony of remembrance every November.

At the same time work was beginning on the great memorial cemeteries in France where millions of war dead were re-buried (the Commonwealth War Graves Commission today maintains 1.2 million UK and Commonwealth graves). Once more Luytens was one of the architectural driving forces, while Sir Reginald Blomfield (who also designed the Menin Gate monument unveiled in 1927) contributed the 'cross of sacrifice', a bronze broadsword imposed on a tall Latin cross, used widely in the British cemeteries in France and the design precursor to many of the village memorials in the UK.

The largest of these British commemorative war graves was the Thiepval memorial to the missing of the Somme, situated north-east of Amiens. Opened on 31 July 1932 by the Prince of Wales, it remains the largest British war memorial in the world, containing the names of 73,357 British and South African men who have no known grave and who fell on the Somme between July 1916 and March 1918. It is 150 feet high, built of stone and pink brick, and dominating the surrounding area. It was again the work of Lutyens. Lutyens also contributed the 'Stone of Remembrance', with words from the *Wisdom of Sirach*** 'Their name liveth for evermore' (popularised by Rudyard Kipling), which was placed in cemeteries of more than 1,000 graves. Kipling was also responsible for the headstones' legend for the many, many bodies for whom identification was impossible: 'A Soldier of the Great War - Known Unto God'.

The navy too needed its equivalent of Thiepval. The great Chatham Naval Memorial was one of three built to recognise those of the navy who had no known grave, the majority of deaths having occurred at sea where no permanent memorial could be provided. An Admiralty committee recommended that the three manning ports in Great Britain - Chatham, Plymouth and Portsmouth - should each have an identical memorial in the form of an obelisk, which would also serve as a leading mark for shipping. The memorials were designed by Sir Robert Lorimer, a Scottish architect of the 'Arts and Crafts' school who had already designed the Scottish National War Memorial at Edinburgh Castle, with sculpture by Henry Poole (who had worked in the army school of camouflage during the conflict). The Chatham memorial, which contains 8,515 names, was unveiled by the Prince of Wales (the future King Edward VIII) on 26 April 1924. It is made of Portland stone with bronze plaques for the names of the fallen. Steps lead up to a plinth and projecting corners with reclining lions, beneath a stepped base to the obelisk, which again has a stepped top to an decorative finial with ship's prows corners and bronze supports to a copper ball. Here the names of many of *Formidable*'s men are recorded, *Formidable* being a 'Chatham ship'.

In the UK there was no organised plan for the building of

**The Book of the All-Virtuous Wisdom of Joshua ben Sira*, commonly called the *Wisdom of Sirach* or simply *Sirach*, and also known as *The Book of Ecclesiasticus* or *Siracides* or *Ben Sira*, is a work of ethical teachings from approximately 200-175 BC written by the Jewish scribe Shimon ben Yeshua ben Eliezer ben Sira of Jerusalem and discovered in 1896 by a pair of Scottish women in Old Cairo.

local war memorials but civic leaders, mayors, squires, parish councils all took their own separate initiatives and war memorials began to cover the land like a rash. Some were architecturally significant, others were wholly meretricious, many were very similar, coming from firms of stone masons who turned them out wholesale, under the (often very distant) influence of designs by Blomfield, Lutyens and the more avant garde Eric Gill and Alfred Gilbert.

Perhaps unsurprisingly, a common motif was the chivalric. St Georges holding upturned swords, angels carrying soldiers in their arms, medieval knights in dreamy reverie can still be seen in many churchyards and village squares. And if Blomfield's cross of sacrifice was too expensive, a simple Celtic cross sufficed for many more.

The Hall of Memory in Centenary Square, Birmingham serves as an example of the elaborate and expensive. Built in 1922–23 at a cost of £60,000 and funded by public donation, it resembles nothing less than a Palladian villa or the Temple of the Winds in Athens. It commemorates the 12,320 men of Birmingham who lost their lives. Made from Portland stone, the foundation block was laid by the Prince of Wales on 12 June 1923 and it was opened by Prince Arthur of Connaught in July two years later before a crowd of 30,000. There are four statues around the exterior representing the army, the navy, the air force, and women's services and the interior features three carved bas-relief plaques representing three tableaux: Call (departure to war); Front Line (fighting); Return (arrival home of the wounded).

One of the best of the 'St George' inspired memorials was made by the sculptor Charles Leonard Harwell and was unveiled in Eldon Square, Newcastle upon Tyne by Earl Haig in 1923. It portrays, in bronze, a mounted knight in armour (a pastiche of the fourteenth century) reaching down to spear a sinuous dragon, all standing on a six-feet-high plinth. Panels front and back depict an idealised female 'Justice' with her scales, tempered by 'Mercy' and 'Peace' in diaphanous flowing robes. It was so successful that a second casting was made to stand outside St John's Wood Church, Marylebone. The St George equestrian bronze is every bit a chivalric figure, straight out of the imaginings of Burne-Jones and his followers and representing an idealised courtly Camelot.

The town of Crewe lost 700 men in the Great War but the authorities were slow to decide to erect a memorial, with cost concerns to the fore. Eventually it was decided to meet the costs by public subscription with the hope that the London and North Western Railway, the town's principal employer, would be a generous donor. £1,600 was eventually raised, of which the railway company gave £600, and in 1924 an Alfred Gilbert-esque bronze statue of Britannia, holding a trident and standing on shattered chains, was erected in the market square. Mounted on a pedestal, itself on a rectangular base, the names of the dead were inscribed on bronze tablets around the fundament, the Villiers-Russell twins among them. A plaque on the pedestal reads:

> This statue was placed to commemorate the men of Crewe who seeking the welfare of their country gave their lives in so doing and are now resting in and beyond the seas.

Among the largest and tallest memorials in the country was the Nicholson memorial in Leek, Staffordshire. It was unusual in that it was paid for by a private individual, not by public donation, and was presented to the town in 1925 by Sir Arthur Nicholson in memory of his son Lieutenant Basil Lee Nicholson (killed in action at Ypres in 1915, at the age of 24) and all the other local men who died in the war. It is a 90-feet-high tower with a rusticated base, four clock faces and five bells and is clad with Portland stone around a red brick inner core. The Birmingham Guild of Artists designed the dedicatory and memorial tablets. The cost of building it was a substantial £16,000, some £823,000 in today's money.

By contrast the village of Lamport, Northants, has a simple Celtic cross inscribed 'In undying memory of the men of this parish who fell in the Great War, 1914–19'. Beneath the cross are engraved the names of the fallen, among them that of Noel Loxley, whose birthplace Lamport was. And in St Mary's churchyard, Northchurch, another almost identical Celtic cross was erected, dedicated on 6 March 1920 by Rear Admiral Lionel Halsey, Comptroller and Treasurer to the Prince of Wales, the Prince being patron of St Mary's church, beneath which are engraved the names of all three Loxley brothers in this, Noel's home parish.

And so the names of the men of *Formidable* began to appear on stone and brass and paper, and provided places for grief to be expressed, memories to be mulled over and loss to be annealed. For those left behind this was, perhaps, a cold comfort.

17

Those Left Behind

They shall grow not old, as we that are left grow old:
(Laurence Binyon, *For the Fallen*)

The deaths of nearly 600 men and officers with the loss of *Formidable* clearly left behind many dependents – wives, parents, children – who were now without husband, carer or father – or money. For officers, marriage was not actively encouraged in the Vicwardian navy (the saying was that an officer married was an officer marred). Postings overseas could last for up to four years and be followed immediately by another one. Wives might be subject to long periods alone. Nonetheless most officers did marry, as did Loxley and Ballard. And as officers largely came from the landed and/or moneyed classes their loss, while tragic to their relatives, was not necessarily financially catastrophic. Noel Loxley, for example, left property worth £13,296 gross (£1.17million at today's values) and personal assets of £3,500 (£305,000 today).[1]

For the lower deck, marriage was the norm and, of course, many of the crew of *Formidable* had been reservists, called up for the July 1914 manoeuvres and subsequently kept at their posts. They were fishermen, coastguards, enthusiastic amateurs and boys. Most of the men were both married and

174

expecting to be away from home and job for only two weeks or so. In any case, these were jobs which, generally, gave little scope for savings.

Now their dependents were thrown upon the mercy of the state – but that mercy did not extend very far in 1915 and the sources of potential succour were both small and complex. The Vicwardians regarded the poor as in some way deserving of their plight, taking the Biblical view that 'you will always have the poor among you'[2], splitting them into the 'deserving' poor, who found themselves in poverty through no fault of their own, and the 'undeserving' poor, who were unwilling to seek out work and were considered to be the next thing to a criminal. Poor relief was provided from parish funds only through the draconian ministrations of the workhouse, governed by local boards of guardians and (from 1871) under the central aegis of the Local Government Board. Poor relief was a direct cost to the local parish (through the rate system) and therefore it was considered appropriate to keep the conditions and costs of the workhouse and poor relief such that one would have to be severely in need of help to request assistance. Workhouse inmates or poor relief recipients lost most of their free rights – for example, until 1918 acceptance of poor relief disqualified the recipient from voting. Perhaps unsurprisingly, at the beginning of the twentieth century it was estimated that 25% of the population were living in poverty and 10% were living below the subsistence level. The major reason for extreme poverty was found to be the loss of a major breadwinner.

It might be noted that the navy provided a means for local Boards of Poor Law Guardians to literally 'ship' indigent boys off their books. In the Vicwardian era there were some twelve training ships which existed to take boys otherwise destined for the workhouse and train them for royal or merchant navy employment. Such a course was heavily promoted by the Local Government Board in the early twentieth century, although the Guardians themselves seem to have shown some reluctance to use training ships for boys in their care. At the beginning of 1911, for example, the national total of Poor Law boys placed on the ten ships then available was only 453. The fact that the cost of maintaining the boys on these ships was 8 or 9 shillings a week might have played a part in this reluctance.

Nonetheless it was seen as a good solution to indigence by many. A paper read by one Geoffrey Drage at the Central Poor Law Conference in February 1904 enthused about the virtues of training ships: 'The so-called stigma of pauperism is removed, and the boys are sent out into the world with a profession of national utility ... [in the navy] at the age of 40 [he can] secure a pension of over £50 for life.'[3]

Indeed a previous *Formidable* had been such a training ship, leased from the Admiralty in 1869 in a scheme financed by several Bristol businessmen who were concerned about the significant number of urchins and street arabs wandering the city's streets. She was moored at Portishead, could take up to 350 boys and was only withdrawn from service by the Admiralty early in 1906 after being damaged by gales.

As late as 1914 such training ship schemes were still being promoted. On 31 January the Duke of Teck (brother-in-law of the king) wrote to the *Daily Telegraph* appealing for funds to establish a training ship (to be named after the late President of the Ragged Schools Union, the Marquis of Northampton) which would take 300 'blind alley boys' and train them for 'the Navy, Army or the Colonies'. The navy had provided the former *Sharpshooter* to be moored at Temple Pier on the Thames for the purpose.

For other means of income, some trades offered 'Friendly Societies' which allowed members to 'self-insure' against hard times. One of the more exotic was the Cricketers' Friendly Society, founded in 1857, to which members contributed a guinea a year (plus the proceeds of certain exhibition matches) and in return could draw down a pound or two a week when destitute.

The position began to change with the introduction of a basic state pension – the 'Old Age Pension' – by the Liberal government of H.H. Asquith in January 1909. The Act provided for a non-contributory old age pension for persons over the age of 70. It paid a weekly pension of 5 shillings a week (7s 6d for married couples) to the half a million or so who were eligible. The level of benefit had been deliberately set low to encourage workers to also make their own provision for retirement. In order to be eligible they had to be earning less than £31 10s per year, and had to pass a 'character test'; only those with a 'good character' could receive a pension. Potential recipients also had to have been a UK resident for at least 20 years and people who hadn't worked their whole life were disbarred. Also among the excluded were those in receipt of poor relief, lunatics in asylums, persons sentenced to prison for ten years after their release, persons convicted of drunkenness (at the discretion of the court) and any person who was guilty of 'habitual failure to work' according to their ability. Given that the average life expectancy in 1914 was 51.5 for men and 55.35 for women, the likely benefit of the Act on elderly people robbed of their sons' support by the war was likely to be low.

The introduction of old age pensions did not command universal approval. One newspaper commented 'on this [the navy] our existence as a nation and our commercial and financial position depend, even before old age pensions. It is still true that the Navy is our "all in all".'[4]

The navy had traditionally paid pensions for death in service out of the funds of the Commissioners of Greenwich Hospital. But these were in the form of gratuities and were not for life. For example, an order in council of 1863 fixed the gratuity at one year's salary, to be paid by the aforesaid commissioners, to widows of men killed while on active service. This arrangement continued, with minor changes, up until the outbreak of war. At that point the basic salary of an able seaman was 1s 8d per day or £30 per annum (1s 11d after 6 years' service). A lieutenant, by contrast, earned 10 shillings a day (£182 per annum). These rates may be contrasted with those of an elementary school teacher or steam engine driver at the same time of around 48 shillings per week, or £124 16s per annum.

At the beginning of the conflict, responsibility for naval pensions for the widows, children and dependents of those killed still lay with the Admiralty, through the Greenwich Hospital fund. But this was superseded in November 1915 by the establishment of the Royal Patriotic Fund Corporation, enabled by the Naval and Military War Pensions Act in which, for the first time, the state – under the pressure of the mass slaughter on the Western Front – recognised its responsibility for the welfare of the war wounded and dead. Monies were disbursed through no fewer than 1,200 local committees and were derived from voluntary funds (i.e. including those previously held by the navy and army for pension purposes) with some government help. Unsurprisingly this was a cumbersome and inefficient method of providing relief.

The Act provided that for 26 weeks after the notification of death, separation allowance would continue to be paid, and then for a further 26 weeks a pension payment would be made. This was around 10 shillings per week for dependent parents, an amount equivalent to the previous weekly salary of the deceased for wives and 10 shillings each for dependent children. Payment was discretionary and after the full 52 (26+26) weeks had expired recipients were thrown onto their own resources. If a beneficiary was in receipt of an old age pension payment then the death in service pension was proportionately reduced. For comparison it should be noted that the average agricultural labourer's cash wage in 1914 was around 16 shillings and 9 pence per week. The average

UK wage in 1914 lay between 26 and 30 shillings per week. By 1917 a bus driver would earn 70 shillings and a cleaner 40, largely due to manpower shortages.

It can therefore be readily seen that the death of a loved one, apart from the obvious emotional upset, was also a financial calamity. The wives and children of *Formidable*'s fallen were placed on the very edge of penury. And this seemed a lesser priority than financial loss due to the disruption of war. An interesting insight into such attitudes to the war was given at the Coroner's Inquest in Brixham into the death of Stoker Alexander Chantrell. The coroner insisted that a rider be added to the verdict to the effect that fishermen who brought in the dead bodies of sailors should be compensated for the financial loss due to leaving the fishing grounds. He suggested that the trawlermen had suffered a loss of £10–15 and that they should make a claim on the Admiralty for that amount, via the Chief Coastguard. The skipper should, the coroner noted, 'make his claim and the jury rider would support it'.[5] The *Darlington and Stockton Times* further noted that if there was not compensation then 'the bodies might be left floating about in the Channel and not be brought to port'.[6] It was apparently not enough that the dead man and his mates had given their lives, in part, in protection of the fishermen's right to be out fishing at all!

A Ministry of Pensions was created and came into being on 15 February 1917. It took over administration of pensions including those already granted since 4 August 1914, and tinkering with the level of payment continued until the end of the war. Thus by 1918 the standard parliamentary pension for war widows had reached 13 shillings and 9 pence (going up to 21s 3d for a warrant officer class 1). Children under 16 attracted payments of 5 shillings for the first child, 4s 3d for the second, 3s 4d the third, and 2s 6d thereafter. By way of comparison, the average wage of an agricultural worker, traditionally the lowest paid of workers in the UK, had risen to 30 shillings and 6 pence. This placed dependents in a slightly better position but was still no bed of roses.

War pensions were made a statutory right on 19 August 1919. Before then the claim to a pension was as 'a matter of grace', i.e. discretionary. The claim for pension had to be made within seven years after the date of discharge/death or within seven years after 23 August 1921, whichever was the earlier date.

The widow of a soldier, sailor or airman who had been killed in the war, or who died in consequence of his service within seven years of being wounded or removed from duty, was entitled to a pension of 20 shillings a week, or if she had children or was over 40, 26 shillings and 8 pence a week. For children under 16, the first child attracted 10 shillings, the second child 7s 6d, and 6 shillings thereafter for each child after the second.

Stoker George Murphy of the *Formidable*, a Dover-born reservist aged 42 when he died, had left a wife and six children. From 1919 his widow received a total of 68 shillings and 2 pence a week in widows and dependents' pension. But she had seven mouths to feed and a roof to be kept over their heads.

Special grants were also available. For example, where a widow or child was suffering from prolonged illness causing necessary additional expense which could not be met out of present income, a sickness grant not exceeding 10 shillings per week could be granted.

Finally, remarriage immediately cancelled the pension benefits, which given the shortage of available men after the carnage of the war was possibly not a great disadvantage.

That none of this was a generous settlement can be seen by the typical family weekly expenditure budget of the immediate post war years. Rent 12s 6d, light and cooking 3 shillings, coal 2s 6d, hire-purchase furniture 5 shillings; with no food, clothing or amusement this was already a total of 23 shillings.[7] By way of another comparison, the Marylebone Cricket Club (MCC) issued a new 'tariff' for cricket payments in 1919. It specified that an 'amateur' could receive 30 shillings per day in expenses, an umpire £10 per match and a professional player up to £20 per match. Had he survived the war, the deceased seaman might now be expecting, including marriage separation allowance, a payment of some 61 shillings per week before good conduct payments which can be compared with the starting weekly wage for a police constable in the early 1920s, for example, of 70 shillings or that of an agricultural worker in 1921 of 37 shillings.*

Many women had of course obtained the vote in 1918, influenced in part by a long and often violent campaign by the Suffragette movement. Only 58% of the adult male population was eligible to vote before 1918. But the fact that only men who had been resident in the country for 12 months prior to a general election were entitled to vote effectively disenfranchised a large number of soldiers and sailors who had been serving overseas in the war. Most politicians believed this to be untenable and, with a general election imminent, they were persuaded to extend the vote to all men.

Women were a different matter but their contribution to the war effort, their mobilisation through the suffragette movement and the changing political landscape through the rise of the Labour party, all advanced the cause of enfranchisement. As a result, parliament passed the 1918 Representation of the People Act which allowed women over the age of 30 who met a property qualification to vote.**

---

*However, naval pay was reduced by between 10% and 25% as part of government cost cutting, leading directly to the Invergordon Mutiny by some of the Atlantic Fleet in September 1931.

**The 1918 franchise gave the vote to women aged 30 or over who were householders or the wives of householders together with women who were university graduates or occupied property where the rent was more than £5 per annum.

Although 8.5 million women met this criterion, it only represented 40% of the total population of women in the UK. But it was a start.

In introducing the bill to parliament the Home Secretary George Cave noted:

> War by all classes of our countrymen has brought us nearer together, has opened men's eyes, and removed misunderstandings on all sides. It has made it, I think, impossible that ever again, at all events in the lifetime of the present generation, there should be a revival of the old class feeling which was responsible for so much, and, among other things, for the exclusion for a period, of so many of our population from the class of electors. I think I need say no more to justify this extension of the franchise.[8]

How wrong he was.

The same act abolished property and other restrictions to the franchise for men, and extended the vote to all men over the age of twenty-one. Additionally, men in the armed forces could vote from the age of nineteen. The electorate was thus increased from eight to twenty-one million people, but there was still huge inequality between women and men which was not finally removed until the Equal Franchise Act of 1928.

It is worth noting that had women been enfranchised in 1918 on the same basis as men, many believe that they would have been in the majority because of the loss of men in the war. This is a possible explanation for the qualifying age for women of 30 being settled upon. This change in the electorate produced a Conservative landslide at the election and a terminal split in the Liberal party, but Lloyd George remained prime minister in a coalition government.

As those left behind entered the 1920s they also confronted a world of increasing unemployment, rising to 2 million in

1921, frequent strikes in the coal, transport and power industries (35 million days were lost to strike action in 1919 and a further 29 million in 1920), falling levels of export trade and the onrushing Great Depression. Lloyd George had promised the returning servicemen a 'land fit for heroes'.[9] But it was no promised land for the relicts of the dead of *Formidable*.

Unemployment stayed stubbornly at around 10–12% throughout the 1920s, which may be compared with the rate in 1914 of 3.3%. Strike followed strike, culminating in the General Strike of 1926. The great American Wall Street Crash of 1929 spread depression around the developed world. Even in 1939 there were still 1.35 million men unemployed in Britain.

For the women and children of the *Formidable* men the war had at least provided some potential for paid employment to supplement any war death pension due. Women had taken a greater role in the workplace for the first time during the war, particularly in the armament and munitions industries (the 'munitionettes') where over 800,000 were employed. The number of women in paid employment rose from 3.27 million in 1914 to 4.93 million in 1918, a statistic which takes no account of the transfer of employment from domestic service to industries such as engineering, transport and agriculture. But as the war ended, with the men returning from the front, and with massive unemployment, these opportunities disappeared and working women were seen as doing a man out of a job. 'Our gallant girls' as the newspapers had lauded them during the conflict were now criticised as 'pin money girls'. In November 1918, some 6,000 women sacked as munition workers by the Woolwich Arsenal demonstrated at the Houses of Parliament with the slogan 'Shall Peace Bring Us Starvation?'. Throughout the twenties and thirties it was commonplace for an employer to dismiss a woman employee when they married, as they were seen as taking a man's job and should be at home looking after their husband. Such sackings were particularly commonplace in the local authorities. Any *Formidable* widows who had been lucky enough to find work would soon have lost it with the advent of peace.

An unemployment insurance act had been passed in 1920. It provided for a weekly 'dole' payment of approximately one-third of the national minimum wage for 39 weeks to over 11 million workers – practically the entire civilian working population except domestic servants, farm workers, railroad men, and civil servants. Funded in part by weekly contributions from both employers and employed, it gave weekly payments of 15 shillings for unemployed men and 12 shillings for unemployed women. A family of five received 23 shillings a week. But, as already noted, these payments were far from generous and provided subsistence living at best. The act was regularly amended as its provisions became more and more onerous on government. In 1921, for example, under-18s were mandated to receive less than those over that age and it was decreed that only those 'seeking work' were eligible. This test was rigorously applied. Between 1925 and 1928 some 1.7 million applications for assistance were refused.

'Hunger marches' had started in 1920, the largest coming in 1922 when men from all quarters of the country, but especially the north, marched on Trafalgar Square in protest against the lack of both work and assistance. There had been a brief economic boom in 1918–20 as the end of the war released pent-up consumer demand, but the erection of tariff barriers across the world, the retreat of the United States behind a tariff wall and the decline of Britain's largest export industry, textiles, all served to cause a rapid fall in demand for British goods and exports, on which the economy depended. By 1921 UK exports had declined by 47.9% against the immediate pre-war levels. There was no work and little assistance.

Wesley H. Wright had joined the navy at the age of 16 in 1908 and by the outbreak of war was serving on *Formidable* as an able seaman. He had been one of the lucky ones plucked from the sea by *Topaze*. He was a rarity for a sailor in disliking tattoos, but to avoid ribbing he had had a butterfly tattooed on the top of each foot. Subsequently he served with the mine layer HMS *Abdiel* and after the war, although he remained an able seaman all his service, he had the prestige position of crewing the admiral's barge for Doveton Sturdee and then Hugh Evan-Thomas when they were successively CinC Nore, finally being discharged from the navy in 1922. The years after his discharge demonstrate some of the problems faced by the survivors in the post war period. Wesley had married his childhood sweetheart Ada in 1917 and in 1918 they had twins. He, his wife, the children and his sister-in-law and her husband all lived with his wife's mother in a two-bedroom flat in west London. In 1920 Wesley added a daughter to the already grossly overcrowded apartment. He managed to get a job with the post office in 1924 and a year later Wesley, his wife and three children finally contrived to get a tenancy on a ground floor council built and owned maisonette in W10. Nonetheless, Ada and her mother still had to take in washing to make ends meet. It was not, perhaps, the 'land fit for heroes' that Wesley had been promised.

And men returning from the sea or the trenches found their world changed. Women had got a taste for work and its benefits, they had gained the vote, in some households they were now the major breadwinner. The subservient role wives and girlfriends had played before the war was changing and many men, disillusioned by the empty promises of the politicians, shocked by the slaughter they had seen and participated in, and unable to find remunerative and satisfying work, began to doubt their place in the order of things. Rates of depression and mental health problems rose significantly.

Things got no better in the 1930s. The economy was stuck

in a depression. By the start of 1933 unemployment among those workers covered by unemployment insurance was 22.8% and 3 million men were unemployed.

To make matters worse, the Great War had wiped out a generation of men of marriageable age (by 1919 the number of women in the UK outnumbered men by 1.9 million – our 'surplus girls', according to the *Daily Mail*). For the many bereaved wives of the *Formidable* there was limited opportunity to find love and, perhaps more importantly, support for their family again.

When *Formidable* went down it was more than a naval disaster. It was the ruination of nearly 600 families. Broken hearts, broken lives, broken dreams.

18

Postscript

What's memory but the ash
That chokes our fires that have begun to sink?
(W.B. Yeats, The Countess Cathleen)

People

Commander Ballard's daughter Margaret, a daughter he never saw, married her second cousin Arthur Charles Corry Gotto of Bangor, County Down. She died aged 89 in 2003. They had two children: Margaret, who died a spinster aged only 52, and Charles, who did wed, and died aged 67. Violet, Ballard's wife of only 18 months, never remarried and died in 1969 aged 78.

Noel Loxley's wife Gladys did not remarry either. She died in 1940 at the age of 57.

Not all the wives left behind were as loyal to the memory of their late husbands however. Fleet Paymaster Ling's wife Gwladis, granddaughter of the 2nd Baron Erskine, remarried in 1924 at 46 and lived to the ripe old age of 82. She donated Ling's greatcoat, sword and medals to the Brixham Heritage Museum.

Peter Loxley had married Elizabeth Lavender Dawney in 1938. He was 33 and she only 24. They went on to have two children, the first of whom, Elizabeth Patricia, was born at the outbreak of the second war. She went to Oxford University (Somerville) where she met Thomas Henry Bingham and went on to marry him in 1963. In 1996 he became Baron Bingham of Cornhill and Lord Justice of Appeal, a post he held for four years.

Elizabeth's mother, who preferred to be known as Lavender, died in 1995. As part of the settlement of death duties the Victoria and Albert Museum received an English casket, wooden with embroidered silk panels and five secret drawers, and dating to approximately the 1660s. The casket had reputedly been made by the Smart family to commemorate a visit to Norcott Court by Charles II and had been part of the inheritance of Noel Loxley's grandmother, also Elizabeth.

Noel's widow Gladys (née Brooke-Hunt) had lost her father the day after the sinking of *Formidable*. Her younger brother Robert Cecil joined the RAF and achieved the rank of captain but died in 1923 at only 24. The Brooke-Hunts are all buried in Upton St. Leonard's Churchyards, Glos, father Arthur Ernest and his wife under one memorial ('Thine eyes shall see the King in his beauty'); brother Robert and Uncle Robert Henry (who had been a Lt. Col. in the 72nd Seaforth Highlanders) beneath another ('The peace of God which passeth all understanding'). But Gladys is not among them.

William Pillar's involvement with the war did not end with his rescue of the *Formidable*'s survivors. On 28 November 1916 he and the rest of the Brixham fishing fleet were attacked off the south Devon coast by a German submarine. *Provident* was the first ship to come under fire from the surfaced vessel's gun; the initial shot brought down her jib and a second cut her topsail halyards. Pillar and his crew hastily launched a small boat and fled as twenty further shots and finally some sort of grenade from close range completely destroyed his beloved trawler. The Germans next turned their fire on Pillar and his men in their tiny craft but

188

fortunately missed. They then focused their attention on other members of the fleet, sinking seven in total. Dan Taylor told the local paper of a strange premonition of disaster; 'You know the Provident didn't want to go to sea. She seemed to hang back from going out. We had to make her go round the Berry.' Pillar added that the ship's clock had 'acted the goat and wouldn't go'.[1]

In August 1940, as the guns of a new and different war were again sounding across France, the Royal National Lifeboat Association presented Captain Pillar with a certificate of thanks, recording that he 'was second Coxswain for seven and three-quarter years and a member of the Torbay lifeboat for sixteen and three-quarter years during which period the lifeboat rescued 136 lives from shipwreck. The Committee of Management are glad to place on record this testimony of his personal participation in the Lifeboat service'. The certificate can still be seen in Brixham lifeboat house.

Pillar lived to be 87 and was a familiar figure on the quay at Brixham, where elderly marines and sailors would sometimes come up to him and shake his hand in gratitude. He lives on today in his native Brixham, immortalised in street names – Pillar Avenue, Pillar Close and Pillar Crescent, all in the vicinity of the cricket ground – and by an English Heritage Blue Plaque, erected in the harbour area in 2010.

Places

The war memorial at Northchurch, Loxley's home parish, did not survive the test of time. In the early 1960s a major crack was discovered. To prevent a possible accident and to preserve the names inscribed on the memorial's base the parishioners decided to remove the cross and re-erect it on a new limestone plinth. The original base was moved a few yards to a position nearer the churchyard wall.

John Loxley's Norcott Court still exists. Noel had rented it out to one Edward Bowill and after Loxley's death it passed through the hands of the Tuke and Davidson families. Stanley Baldwin was a frequent guest after his wife died and Winston Churchill used it as an alternative meeting place to nearby Chequers during the Second World War.

Ships

Provident was finally replaced in 1924 by a vessel built with a government grant awarded in recognition of the heroic rescue. She fished out of Brixham for another ten years before being sold to a wealthy American and converted into a private yacht. In time she returned home, was restored and now operates as part of a small sailing holiday fleet, still based in Devon.

Formidable's twin sisters had contrasting fortunes. HMS *Irresistible*, having served in Fleet with her sisters, was sent as part of the ill-fated Dardanelles campaign force, taking part in the bombardment of the Turkish forts guarding the straits. On 18 March 1915 she struck a mine, which caused severe damage and killed around 150 of her crew. Without power, she began to drift into the range of Turkish guns. Attempts to tow her failed, she was abandoned with most of the remaining crew having been successfully evacuated, and she sank under gunfire. HMS *Implacable* also served in the Channel Fleet and went to the Dardanelles, surviving the experience. Apart from a brief spell in England in March/April 1916 for a refit, she remained in the Mediterranean until June 1917, supporting first the Italian navy and then the French navy. She returned to England to be laid up until March 1918 and then served as a depot ship for the Northern Patrol. Decommissioned at the end of the war, she was sold for scrap in 1921. She was scrapped in Germany, oddly enough.

For many years the old lady *Formidable* herself lay on the sea bed, easily accessible from the Dorset and Devon coast, prey for divers, souvenir hunters and salvage merchants, the last resting place of nearly 600 men regularly disturbed by intruders. But in 2002 the wreck was designated a war grave under the 1986 Protection of Military Remains Act. It became illegal to disturb or enter her. At last the unquiet grave was given some peace.

The name *Formidable* was not to die out. A new *Formidable* – an Illustrious class aircraft carrier – was launched on 17 August 1939. It was fitting in a way that the name of a battleship of World War I should re-emerge on one of what would prove to be the new capital ships of the second war – carriers. At her launch an accident occurred just before the traditional launching ceremony was due to begin. The wooden cradle supporting the ship collapsed and she careered down the slipway while workmen were still underneath and around the ship. One spectator was killed by flying debris and at least twenty others were injured but the ship was not damaged. From that day, she was nicknamed 'the ship that launched herself'.

This new *Formidable* distinguished herself in the Mediterranean, where she participated in the Battle of Cape Matapan, and later in the Pacific, fighting against the Japanese, where she was badly damaged by a kamikaze attack. Uneconomical to repair properly she was placed in reserve in 1947 (the fate her namesake had faced before the First World War) and sold for scrap in 1953.

The destroyer of the battleship *Formidable*, U-24, somehow outlasted the war and was surrendered with the German fleet in 1918. She and another 175 of her sisters surrendered to Admiral Tyrwhitt at Harwich on 20 November 1918. She was broken up for scrap in 1921.

Tipperary

The wreck survivors had sung *Tipperary* to keep their spirits up while adrift in the raging seas. Most accounts of the tragedy recall this. But why this song and how did it become such a meme of the First World War?

It's a Long Way to Tipperary, to give it its full name, was a British music hall song co-written by Jack Judge and Henry James 'Harry' Williams. Judge had Irish grandparents who hailed from Tipperary although he himself was born in Oldbury, Worcestershire. Williams, who was severely handicapped having fallen downstairs as a child, was from the West Midlands. They began their writing partnership in the 1910s and quickly turned out thirty-two songs, many of which were sung on stage by Judge who was a middle rank music hall performer.

Tipperary was written in 1912 and first performed by Judge on stage at the Grand Theatre, Stalybridge. The Australian-born star Florrie Forde, one of the music hall 'Greats' of the early twentieth century, then took it up and in November 1914 the famous tenor John McCormack recorded it, which helped its worldwide popularity.

The song had been bought by British music publisher Feldman for £5. Harry Williams, who was to die in 1924, was co-attributed as composer. Later in his life when he became very unwell, the company gave him a weekly pension of £1 in recognition of his authorship of one of their biggest selling works.

During the First World War a *Daily Mail* article referenced the Irish regiment the Connaught Rangers singing *Tipperary* as they marched through Boulogne on 13 August 1914. For some reason the song was quickly picked up by other units of the British army and then by all of the armed forces. There are probably two reasons for its adoption by the troops and sailors. First, it was easy to march to. Second, unlike the majority of the songs of previous wars and of the outbreak of this one, it was neither jingoistic nor martial. It is a song of nostalgia and longing, as was the other massively popular song of the war *Keep the Home Fires Burning*, concentrating on the yearning for home.

Jack Judge made further contributions to the war effort in 1915 by writing and singing *Paddy Maloney's Aeroplane* and *Michael O'Leary, V.C.*, both about Irishmen helping the war effort. After the war, as a devoted West Bromwich Albion FC supporter, he also wrote songs in support of them.

There is a bronze statue of Judge in Lord Pendry Square, Stalybridge, depicting a Tommy bending over a seated Jack Judge, and the public library in his home town of Oldbury is named for him. But perhaps Judge's and Williams' biggest legacy was that their song gave two boatloads of storm-tossed sailors the focus, energy and determination to survive.

The survivors

For the sailors whose voices have been heard in this narrative, the future brought mixed blessings. Health and nervous problems proved all too present for some of them.

Tom Walker, who had been discharged 'medically unfit for Naval Service' in April 1915, eventually recovered his health and – eschewing the sea for which he now had an understandable dislike – joined the army in 1917, serving in France and post-revolution Russia (and building rail tracks). In World War II he again served his country, initially with the British Expeditionary Force and later as an Unexploded Bomb Disposal Officer. He died in Padstow in 1970.

The hero of Lyme Bay, Thomas 'Mickey' Carroll, continued to serve as a petty officer, much of his remaining time in the war being at Chatham barracks, until being invalided out of the navy in 1920 with gastritis, possibly an ulcer.

193

Joseph Taplin, who spotted the light of the cinema projector at Lyme, and had been in the service since 1908 when he had joined up from his home in Poplar aged 12, never served again. He was invalided out of the navy just five months after the *Formidable* went down with the diagnosis of a nervous breakdown. Telegraphist George Wilson also never went to sea again and was invalided out in April 1915 with rheumatism and, again, a nervous breakdown, aged only 22.

While nervous disintegration is always terrible, the navy appears to have treated these men better than they could have expected in the army. In the Great War around 80,000 British troops were diagnosed with what became known as 'shell shock', what we now call post-traumatic stress disorder. Many suffered a full nervous collapse. All combatant nations suffered. The Germans called the condition *Kriegsneurose*, but the French refused to recognise that it existed – the French language did not, or would not, legitimise a disorder that could exempt a soldier from what many saw as a holy war, a war in defence of civilisation (which was, of course, defined as France).

For the British, cases of shell shock were interpreted as neither a physical nor a psychological injury, but as simply a lack of moral fibre. Often men suffering from shell shock were put on trial, and even executed, for military crimes resulting from their condition, including desertion and cowardice. Commanders did not wish to recognise the problem as a medical one for fear it would become an 'easy way out'. Because of this lack of medical recognition shell shock was not, in itself, an admissible defence in cases of court martial and men were executed who would today be diagnosed with post-traumatic stress disorder. The prejudice against recognising the problem as a psychological one continued after the war. In his testimony to the post-war Royal Commission examining shell shock, Lord Gort (known as 'Tiger', himself a

194

fearless man and winner of the VC and MC) said that shell shock was a weakness that was not found in good units.

There were so many officers and men suffering from shell shock that nineteen British military hospitals were completely turned over to the treatment of such cases. Ten years after the war 65,000 ex-servicemen were still receiving treatment for shell shock in Britain. Thus, although Taplin and Wilson broke down under the effects of the disaster, they could perhaps consider themselves lucky to be able to leave the navy.

Torpedo Gunner Daniel Horrigan, who had received his warrant rank only eight months before the sinking, suffered cruelly at the hands of capricious fate. He was admitted to Haslar Hospital in April 1915 with tuberculosis of the lung, was pensioned off three months later as physically unfit and died in September of the following year, aged just thirty. The seas and the strain took a big toll of these men.

Others were luckier. Master at Arms Cooper was demobbed and pensioned in 1919 and joined the Royal Fleet Reserve. Herbert Bing, another of the heroes of the Lyme Regis boat, retired from the service in 1922 with a pension. Eddison Wheatley, the swimmer from Morley in Yorks, reached the rank of leading seaman and served until 1927, joining the RFR two years later. He had passed his petty officer exams three years before leaving the navy but never received the promotion they prefigured. Alfred Booth stayed on until 1928. John Cowan, saved from certain death by the Pilot Boat Inn's dog Lassie, also stayed on and was demobbed two years after the war's end.

Jack Fisher was transferred from *Topaze* to HMS *Pembroke*, the shore barracks at Chatham, until August 1915 when he went to sea again with the 12-inch monitor HMS *General Craufurd*, where he remained for the rest of the war. He rated Petty Officer in 1920 and stayed on, serving ashore and on battleships, until his discharge in 1927. Come the second world conflict he signed on again, despite being in his mid-forties, and served as Chief Petty Officer on board the armed merchant cruiser HMS *Ausonia*, where he was gazetted with the British Empire Medal for gallantry in July 1941.

James Connor chose to forfeit his naval pension so that he could transfer to the New Zealand Division* in 1920, after service with the NZ cruisers *Dunedin* and *Canterbury* the year before. He emigrated to seek a new life as far away from England as he could get, perhaps foreseeing the lack of chances for gainful employment in Britain in the 1920s.

As for the marines, Ernest Hunt was discharged in 1919 with the rank of corporal and John Mitchell was invalided out in the same rank a year later.

Police Sergeant James Stockley stayed in the force for another four years after his moment of fame before retiring at the age of 42.

Having survived his premature 'death', Midshipman Ivor MacGregor went on to serve in Q-ships, in which service he was wounded in May 1917 and awarded the Distinguished Service Cross (DSC). Married the same year, he survived the war and was demobbed in 1919, remaining in the RNR and joining the Orient Line as an officer. He became a pilot on the Suez Canal in 1924 and eventually reached the RNR rank of commander, continuing to serve on the canal at the outbreak of the second war and briefly becoming the British Military Attaché in Turkey. He died in 1952 at the age of 58.

Twelve officers survived the sinking; six midshipmen, three lieutenants, two assistant paymasters (equivalent to a sub-lieutenant in rank) and a lieutenant commander. The

---

*Technically the New Zealand Division of the Royal Navy between 1921 and 1941, funded largely from Wellington, under the overall command of the China Station and based in New Zealand.

Gieves life preservers no doubt played a part in their survival. They were to enjoy contrasting future fortunes.

Midshipmen Hurd-Wood, Pelly, Agnew, Wynne and Guinness were reassigned on 18 January 1915 and lent to the Australian navy to serve on HMAS *Australia*, an Indefatigable class battlecruiser. But not for them the delights of warm waters and Pacific cruising, for *Australia* was now serving with the Grand Fleet at Scapa. As such they appeared in the Australian Navy List of 1915 and in 1917 they were all promoted to the rank of sub-lieutenant. But their survival did not significantly enhance the navy's gene pool, with one notable exception. Denis Pelly ('plays games well' according to his Admiralty report card) resigned his position in February 1920 after his father had written to the authorities querying his prospects for future progression. Norman Hurd-Wood ('slow but hard-working') was placed on the retired list as a lieutenant in 1923 and was made lieutenant commander in retirement in 1924. Perhaps choosing to reside as far from the sea as possible, he went to live in Switzerland. Walter Agnew made lieutenant in 1919 and retired in 1927 with the rank of lieutenant commander. He re-enlisted in 1938 but was invalided out two years later and died in 1942. However, Trethowan Campbell Trevredyn Wynne made a rather better fist of naval life. He retired first in 1931 as a lieutenant commander (with none other than the future First Sea Lord Dudley Pound writing that he 'would do well in higher ranks') and having been 'mentioned in despatches' in 1919. Remobilised as an acting-captain for the Second World War he distinguished himself at the Battle of Mataplan in 1942, winning the Distinguished Service Cross (DSC) and being awarded the American Legion of Merit before retiring a second time in 1947.

On discharge from *Diamond* (via HMS *Implacable*, sister ship to *Formidable*), Assistant Paymaster Saxton was sent to the most unlikely of hospitals – Highclare House, the model for today's TV series *Downton Abbey* – and home to an orthopaedic hospital established there on the outbreak of war by Almina, Lady Carnarvon. There he was treated for broken bones, shock and hypothermia. He survived the experience and served again in the second great conflict, reaching the rank of paymaster commander.

Of the lieutenants, William Derek Stephens went on to enjoy a successful career, reaching the rank of captain in 1937, serving as Director of the Trade Division at the Admiralty between 1943 and 1945 and taking command of the aircraft carrier *Illustrious* in Pacific waters between July 1945 and early 1947 when he retired. He service earned him honours, the more esoteric of which included the Polish Order Odrodzenia Polski, 3rd class, Commander of the Order of Orange-Nassau and the Legion of Merit, degree of Commander.

Lieutenant (E) Bernard W. Greathed, born in Winnipeg, Manitoba in 1891, was promoted Commander (E) in 1926 and two years later married Beatrix May Davidson, of Scottish birth, in France. There were no children from the marriage but in 1933 Beatrix inherited £120,000 (c. £7.2 million at today's values) which left them very comfortably off. Bernard was promoted Rear-Admiral (E) in 1944, awarded the CB in 1946 and retired to spend time cruising with his wife. He died in Berwick in 1961.

Lieutenant James C.J. Soutter was assigned to a sister ship of his rescuer, the Gem class cruiser HMS *Amethyst*, and served with her in the Dardanelles campaign where he was mentioned in despatches. He transferred to the Australian navy and assumed command of the submarine depot ship HMAS *Platypus*, in which capacity the *Sydney Morning Herald* found him on 25 January 1924 when he helped to welcome the Japanese Admiral Saito and his squadron to Government House, Sydney, as part of a Japanese courtesy visit.

Finally, Lieutenant Henry D. Simonds, who had been commended by Loxley for his work with the boats, retired with the rank of lieutenant-commander to become a Life Member of the Court of the University of Reading on its foundation in 1926. This was perhaps not entirely unexpected as he was a scion of the famous Simonds brewing dynasty whose premises, first as H&G Simonds and later as Courage Barclay and Simonds, dominated the Reading skyline for centuries. His eldest brother was the managing director and another brother rose to be a Law Lord and Lord of Appeal in Ordinary.

Aftermath

Today (2015) there is little to indicate that nearly 600 men lost their lives just twenty miles off the Dorset and Devon coast. The grave of the six sailors who came ashore with the pinnace is just one of many in Lyme Regis cemetery, not even in the correct position according to the cemetery plan. But every remembrance day some citizens of Lyme Regis still honour the six dead sailors with a graveside ceremony. The town's museum has a very small display relating to the disaster, including a boot reputed to be from a *Formidable* sailor, although that is unlikely unless it belonged to a coal trimmer, given that it has a metal toecap. There is no memorial in the parish church or on the Cobb to confirm the point at which the exhausted men staggered ashore.

In Brixham the museum has an even smaller display, just Ling's coat, sword and medals, to mark Pillar's bravery and the sailors' gratitude, although, as has been detailed, Pillar is well commemorated in the town. A picture of *Provident*'s crew even forms part of a montage decorating the side of the fish market, although it is unlikely that any of the passers-by realise its relevance.

In Kent the names on the Chatham Memorial are lost among the many others who died in the succeeding years of the war.

The First World War ground to a halt, exhausted nations leaning on metaphorical crutches, in November 1918 and as the butcher's bill was counted, the loss of nearly 600 men from *Formidable* must have seemed relatively trivial; and more so after a second war less than twenty-five years later. But at the time it mattered and the townsfolk of Brixham and Lyme Regis, exposed to war on their very doorsteps, were able to play a part and recognise the sacrifice of those who were defending them.

The Second World War proved Fisher right and Bayly and his coevals wrong; submarines played a major role and the capital ship became almost a liability under the twin assault of airpower and submarine weapons. Bayly probably came to realise that he had been wrong during his time (successfully) defending the Western Approaches, although he seems to have been reluctant to admit it.

So who was to blame for the disaster? The Admiralty for turning back the destroyers? Bayly for staying out at sea in appalling weather and in waters where submarines had already caused significant losses? Bayly's subordinates for failing to question his decision not to zig-zag? All have their excuses. The Admiralty didn't believe that Bayly could be so stupid as to not take anti-submarine precautions and to stay out at night in dangerous weather and waters. Bayly believed that he would have been told if there were subs around his position; and he did not take submarines seriously anyway. And his captains were culturally unable to question Bayly's orders, both from long custom and training and because of his abrasive personality.

Of course, Bayly was directly to blame for the loss of *Formidable* and the 583 men and boys. But Commander Dewar was correct when he wrote that 'One does not blame the Admiral ... one blames the system which makes it possible for such a man to command.'[2]

In the end it was the system that killed *Formidable* and her men. It was a nineteenth-century command group in a twentieth-century war; an arrogant and closed community which had resisted change and innovation; a set of behaviours which created a culture of slavish obedience to orders and reverence for the past; a political nexus which placed more value on quantity rather than quality of ships.

Who was to blame? It was the navy.

19

Envoi

Never such innocence
Never before or since
(Phillip Larkin, *MCMXIV*)

The self-sacrificing heroism of Loxley and Ballard, Pillar and Stockley might seem odd to a twenty-first-century reader, but to them it was natural. Their personalities were a direct function of their upbringing and the culture and mores with which they grew up. Personal bravery was an expectation; it was inconceivable that a Vicwardian man would behave otherwise. To be considered a coward was social and professional suicide. All of their education, reading and peer pressure emphasised this and they were in the thrall of the chivalric code imagined to pertain in mediaeval and Arthurian times.

The values that they represented – honour, loyalty, obedience, bravery, sacrifice – came to be somewhat derided; now they are lost for ever through a changed political and educational prism which makes it difficult for us today to wholly comprehend their actions. Whether it was Loxley on his bridge with Bruce by his side, Pillar attempting a seemingly impossible rescue or Stockley risking his life to save others on the beach, they knew what was expected of them and how a man should behave. They had certainty and that gave them inner peace and courage.

The First World War began the process of the destruction of this certainty, at least in Britain. By war's end women had entered the workplace in roles traditionally the preserve of men. The electorate had been greatly expanded and now included women and the 'working class'. Deference to power and the aristocratic elite had been eroded (as had the aristocratic elite) and men's roles had started to be defined differently from the previously prevailing ones of breadwinning and bravery.

This process was accelerated by the Second World War and the advent of the feminist thinking of the late 1960s and 70s, and has now reached the point where many men are seemingly uncertain of their role. Are they expected to be brave, macho and drop baby off at nursery? Equal partners in a relationship or principal wage earner? To eat dinner when they come home or to cook dinner when they come home? Couple this confusion with the advent of a society where people believe they have rights but not responsibilities – the very opposite of what Loxley or Pillar believed – and you have a recipe for uncertainty and some might say emasculation. All the characters in this book would be bemused by the world of today.

Assuming such heroes could even be found nowadays, they would quickly be elevated into demi-gods by a fawning media, before that self-same media then turned on them to cut them down with revelations of some personal weakness, true or false, the 'tall poppy' getting its come-uppance. Today experience has taught us to look for some hidden motivation, some personal interest, in such apparently selfless acts of bravery. What's in it for them, we ask, our cynicism fuelled by countless disappointing stories of venal politicians, corrupt policeman or money-obsessed businessmen.

But to apply these modern standards to men like Loxley is

203

to misunderstand the Vicwardian era. It was the last stand of chivalry, the Thermopylaen pass of honour, the prelapsarian Eden of England. The Great War to End All Wars (which failed even in its naming) destroyed this golden fantasy land. An edgier, tougher, more cynical, more self-serving world emerged in which Loxley, Ballard, Pillar, Stockley, and Bing, Carroll and Smithurst too, were increasingly alienated. For the survivors as well as for the dead, it would never be the same again.

Truly, these men were The Last Action Heroes.

Appendices

Appendix 1: The 'Lassie Legend'

Writer Nigel Clarke, in *The Shipwreck Guide to Dorset and South Devon*,[1] believes the Lassie of the Pilot Inn was the original 'Lassie', the dog that inspired so many films and television episodes. According to Clarke, when the sailors heard the story of Lassie and what she did to rescue Cowan they told it again and again to any reporter who would listen, as it was inspirational and heart-warming. Hollywood got hold of the story, and so a star was born.

Another story has it that photographs of Lassie, along with Able Seaman John Cowan, appeared in the newspapers and on postcards. The journalist Eric Knight (a Yorkshireman who had emigrated to America and bred collies on his Pennsylvania ranch) heard of her, and gave her name to the heroine of his 1938 serialised story in the *Saturday Evening Post* (an American weekly magazine), later extended to a novel, *Lassie Come Home*. Knight was killed in a plane crash in Dutch Guiana, serving in the US forces just before the 1943 release of the famous MGM Technicolor film, which was shot in California. Female dogs tend to shed hair when in heat so, unknown to viewers, Pal, the magnificent collie playing Lassie, was male.

However, I believe that both of these stories of Lassie's genesis are gilding the lily. A 'Lassie' appears in literature as early as 1859, in Mrs Elizabeth Gaskell's short story 'The Half-Brothers'. In the story Lassie is described as a female collie with intelligent, apprehensive eyes who rescues two half-brothers who are lost and dying in the snow. When the younger brother can no longer carry on, elder brother Gregory, Lassie's master, ties a handkerchief around Lassie's neck and sends her home. Lassie arrives home, and leads the search party to the boys. When they arrive Gregory is dead, but his younger half-brother is saved. It would thus appear that Gaskell both created the name 'Lassie' for a special dog and defined the archetypical storyline that would keep Lassie in the public eye throughout the twentieth century. It might also explain why the Pilot Inn's collie was so named.

Appendix 2: The Missing Boy

There is a persistent rumour that there was a fifth crew member on board the *Provident* at the time of the rescue – a nine-year-old boy called Leonard Pillar, known to his friends as Cher. Indeed he is depicted in a photograph in the *Daily Graphic* of January 4th showing Pillar, his crew and some of the survivors. He is also reported as present, resplendent in his boy scout uniform, when the king presented Pillar and the crew with their medals. It is suggested that he was on holiday from school and had persuaded his uncle Bill to take him fishing. He helped Dan make the tea for the shivering, exhausted sailors and tried to make them comfortable.

However, apart from the *Daily Graphic* photo noted above, no contemporary or subsequent account of the rescue mentions young Leonard being involved at sea. Possibly this is because, given his age, he should not have been on a working boat. Or possibly he was photographed because he wanted to be part of his uncle's moment of celebrity. In any case, he certainly existed and later became a second Captain

Pillar sailing out of Brixham. He moved to Swansea and in the Second World War won the medal that might have been denied to him as a schoolboy, by shooting down a German plane off Milford Haven.

Appendix 3: Naval Courts of Inquiry

As given in Kings Regulations & Admiralty Instructions – 1913, Chapter XVIII, Courts of Inquiry and Naval Courts.

702. Duties and Powers – The duties of a court of inquiry depend on the instructions which the authority ordering the court may think proper to give. The instructions should always be in writing.

703. Use of Court of Inquiry – A court of inquiry may be used by any officer in command of a fleet or squadron, station, or division of a station, to enable him to arrive at a correct conclusion on any matter upon which he requires to be thoroughly informed, or upon which there may be a question whether it should form the subject of a court-martial.

2. A court of inquiry has no power to award any punishment; it can only recommend. It may, however, be invested with any power, not exceeding that of the convening officer, which may be necessary for the proper conducting of the inquiry, such as calling before it naval witnesses and requiring the production of official papers. It may be re-assembled as often, and with such alterations in its composition as may be directed.

3. It is not a judicial body; it has no power to compel the attendance of civilians as witnesses, nor to examine on oath.

4. It may be required to examine witnesses and record their evidence, without being required to give any opinion; no one before it charged with any offence is bound to make any statement or answer any questions.

5. Members of a court of inquiry are not disqualified to sit

on a court-martial upon the same subject-matter, because they have so acted, but they may be objected to, and the objection allowed by the court, and this contingency is to be considered in selecting the members. So far as may be practicable and consistent with a due regard to this contingency, the president and members should be senior to the person whose conduct is under inquiry.

6. A court of inquiry, unless otherwise ordered, shall sit with closed doors.

7. The person concerned in the result of the inquiry should be present during the whole time that witnesses are being examined, but should he object or refuse to be present, the proceedings are to be carried on in his absence, except in the case provided for in Article 778, clause 3 (f).

8. With the exception provided for in Article 776, clause 3 (f), no person is to be present in the character of a prosecutor, nor is any friend or professional adviser to be allowed to assist any person concerned in the inquiry.

9. Every person about to make a statement or answer a question likely to incriminate himself should be cautioned by the court that what he is about to state may be made use of against him. All such cautions should be recorded in the minutes.

10. If the inquiry should have reference to the loss or hazarding of a ship, the course directed by Article 690, with the exception of taking evidence on oath, is to be pursued.

11. The minutes of the proceedings are to be signed by all the members, and forwarded by the president to the authority ordering the inquiry. In case of difference of opinion on any material point among the members, the grounds of difference are to be fully stated.

704. Disposal of Proceedings – The proceedings are in all cases to be sent to the Commander-in-Chief, who, in the absence of special directions, will exercise his discretion as to forwarding them to the Admiralty.

Appendix 4: St Mary's Church, Northchurch, Ensigns

St Mary's is in the patronage of the Duchy of Cornwall. The original white ensign was presented to St Mary's in 1905 by the Prince of Wales (as Duke of Cornwall, the future George V) on the occasion of the marriage of Captain (later Admiral) Lionel Halsey RN to Morwenna Granville, the daughter of Bevel Granville, the owner of Northchurch Hall.

Fifteen years later this flag was used to cover the newly built Northchurch War Memorial which was unveiled on 6 March 1920, on behalf of the new Prince of Wales (the future Edward VIII), by the now Rear Admiral Halsey who was, at this time, Chief of Staff and Comptroller and Treasurer to the Prince.

Following the ceremony, a replacement flag was given to St Mary's by Edward, Prince of Wales. This was eventually replaced due to its age and condition in 1971 by an ensign donated to the church by then Prince of Wales, Charles, as Duke of Cornwall.

Appendix 5: Propaganda and the Defence of the Realm Act – part two

One of the first significant publications to be produced by the BWPB was the Report on Alleged German Outrages, in early 1915. This pamphlet documented atrocities both actual and alleged committed by the German army against Belgian civilians. A Dutch illustrator, Louis Raemaekers, provided highly emotional drawings which appeared in the pamphlet.

Another of Charles Masterman's early projects was a history of the war to be published as a monthly magazine, for which he recruited John Buchan to head its production. Published by Buchan's own publishers, Thomas Nelson, the first instalment of the *Nelson's History of the War* appeared in February 1915. A further twenty-three editions appeared regularly during the war. Buchan was given the rank of second lieutenant in the Intelligence Corps and provided with the necessary documents to write the work. General Headquarters Staff saw this as very good for propaganda as Buchan's close relationship with Britain's military leaders made it very difficult for him to include any criticism about the way the war was being conducted.

After complaints from the USA the British government decided to look again at how the war was being reported. After a Cabinet meeting on the subject in January 1915, the government decided to change its policy and to allow selected journalists to report the war. Five men were chosen: Philip Gibbs (*Daily Chronicle* and *Daily Telegraph*), Percival Philips (*Daily Express* and *Morning Post*), William Beach Thomas (*Daily Mail* and *Daily Mirror*), Henry Perry Robinson (*The Times* and *Daily News*) and Herbert Russell (Reuters News Agency). Before their reports could be sent back to England, they had to be submitted to C.E. Montague, the former leader writer of the *Manchester Guardian*. Douglas Haig, the British supremo on the Western Front, and on whose staff Buchan also served, regarded these men as just so many aides and troops. He gave them captain's uniforms, drivers, escorts and decent accommodation – in stark contrast to the men actually doing the fighting. Montague ensured that their despatches maintained a high patriotic tone, such that at one point in 1916 Haig invited the group to meet him and praised them with the Englishman's (we shall overlook the fact that he was of Scottish birth) highest compliment: 'Gentlemen, you have played the game like men.'[1] Additionally, over the next three years other journalists such as John Buchan, Valentine Williams, Hamilton Fyfe and Henry Nevinson became accredited war correspondents. But to remain on the Western Front these journalists still had to accept government control over what they wrote.

In May 1916 Masterman decided that he could inject more emotion by recruiting the artist Muirhead Bone, who produced 150 drawing and paintings for the BWPB. When Bone returned to Britain the drawings were a great attraction in portraying a successful British army. However, the increasing level of losses, such as the 57,000 British casualties on the first day of the Somme, July 1st 1916, meant that official news channels began to lose credibility as citizens compared their personal experiences and knowledge. Despite that, in 1917 Masterman sent more artists abroad to paint, including Eric Kennington, William Orpen and William Rothenstein. However there was still a limit to what could be depicted. Paul Nash complained at the limitations of what he could draw, saying, 'I am not allowed to put dead men into my pictures because apparently they don't exist.'

DORA (the Defence of the Realm Act 1914) was used to control civilian behaviour and give wide command to the military and government over resources of transport and production. It was also used to regulate alcohol consumption and food supplies. Among other things, in October 1915 the government announced several measures they believed would reduce alcohol consumption, which was thought to depress productivity. Amazingly, almost risibly, a 'No Treating Order' decreed that people could not buy alcoholic drinks for other people. Public house opening times were also reduced to 12.00 noon to 2.30 pm and 6.30 to 9.30 pm. Before the law was changed, public houses had been able to open from 5 in the morning to 12.30 at night. The same act nationalised the breweries in certain locations considered key, namely Carlisle, Enfield Lock and Cromarty. This control was abolished in 1921 except in Carlisle where nationalised pubs and beer continued for the next 40 years, and to the detriment of the drinker.

DORA was also utilised by the, no doubt misogynistic, authorities to impose, *inter alia*, curfews on women whose husbands were away at the front, and to make it a crime for a woman with venereal disease to have sex with a member of the armed forces.

DORA lapsed at the end of the war but some if its provisions were re-enacted in the Emergency Powers Act of 1920 and used against the IRA in Ireland.

Appendix 6: Loxley's Predecessors

Had Loxley lived he would undoubtedly have gained flag rank, as all of his predecessors in *Formidable* had done. The old girl had eight captains in her lifetime. She had been commissioned by Alexander W. Chisholm-Batten who commanded for three years; he retired in 1907 with the rank of rear admiral. Between 1904 and 1906 her captain was Tomas P Walker, who retired as a rear admiral in 1911 but returned to the colours to help the war effort in 1915, with the effective rank of captain RNR (Royal Naval Reserve), and was awarded the DSO.

1906–7 saw Ernest A. Simons in command. He retired in 1915 with the rank of rear admiral. Herbert Lyon commanded for the next two years and retired before the outbreak of war in 1913, again as a rear admiral. Reginald A. Allenby took charge between 1909 and 1911, retiring in 1915 with flag rank. He too returned to aid the war effort, taking the army rank of lieutenant colonel and acting as an assistant embarkation staff officer. Next was Philip Nelson-Ward, great grandson of Lord Nelson himself. He commanded *Formidable* for a year and retired in 1916 as a rear admiral, but returned as a convoy commodore in 1917 when his ship SS *Bostonian* was torpedoed from under him and sank in six minutes. He survived.

Finally, Drury St. A. Wake was *Formidable*'s captain from 1912 to 1914. He left her to take charge of Cruiser Force E

(11th CS, in the Third Fleet) before becoming Senior Naval Officer, Persian Gulf, as a commodore. He retired as rear admiral in 1917 but returned to the war in the RNR as a commodore second class.

Sources, Notes and Select Bibliography

Sources

Authors are fortunate that in the UK we have a number of high-quality archives run by dedicated and helpful staff and their trustees. The writing of this book has been informed by records held at the following and I should like to thank them all for their assistance:

National Archives, Kew (NA)
Churchill Archive Centre, Churchill College, Cambridge (CAC)
Imperial War Museum, London (IWM)
British Library, London (BL)
National Maritime Museum, Greenwich (NMM)
Museum of the Royal Navy, Portsmouth (MRN)
Belfast Central Library (Evelyn Barrett)
Crewe Library (Kathryn Bate)
Stockton-on-Tees Central Library (Reference Library Staff)
Darlington Library (Katherine Williamson)

Dr Phillip Armitage of the Brixham Heritage Museum and Mr Graham Davies of the Lyme Regis Museum were very generous with their time and I thank them for it.

Any errors are mine alone and I would like to hear of them. *Humanum est errare.*

Notes

Introduction
1. 1801 letter to the Board of Admiralty, quoted in J.S. Tucker, *Admiral the Right Hon The Earl of St Vincent GCB&C, Memoirs*, Richard Bentley, 1844.
2. M. Bostridge, *The Fateful Year*, Viking, 2014.

Chapter 1, The Big Ship
1. Fred T. Jane, *Jane's Fighting Ships of World War I*, Jane's Publishing Company, 1919.
2. C.C. Penrose Fitzgerald, *From Steam to Sail*, E. Arnold, 1922.
3. *Daily Telegraph* January 6 1914.
4. Quoted in D. Wragg, *Royal Navy Handbook 1914-18*, Sutton Publishing, 2006.

Chapter 2, The Captain
1. Loxley Naval Record, National Archives, Kew.
2. ibid.
3. ibid.
4. ibid.
5. ibid.
6. Quoted in, *inter alia*, R. McLaughlin, *The Escape of the Goeben*, Seeley Service, 1974.

Chapter 3, The Quickening Tide
1. B. Tuchman, *The Proud Tower*, Hamish Hamilton, 1966.
2. A.J. Marder, *From the Dreadnought to Scapa Flow*, vol 2, OUP, 1965.

Chapter 4, U-24
1. Letter to Keyes, Keyes papers, British Library.
2. Letter, 12 March 1910, McKenna MSS, Churchill Archive Centre, Churchill College, Cambridge (CAC).

Chapter 5, On Board *HMS Formidable*
1. Scarborough Maritime Heritage Centre.
2. Burton Bradstock online.
3. *Wanganui Chronicle*, 6 January 1915.
4. ibid.

5. *South Devon Herald Express*, November 1979.
6. Scarborough Maritime Heritage Centre.
7. Burton Bradstock online.
8. Scarborough Maritime Heritage Centre.
9. ibid.
10. *Wanganui Chronicle*, 6 January 1915.
11. ibid.
12. Burton Bradstock online.
13. *Wanganui Chronicle*, 6 January 1915.

Chapter 6, The Struggle
1. Quoted in *Belfast Evening Telegraph*, 9 January 1915.
2. *The Adelaide Advertiser*, 4 January 1915.
3. *Brixham Western Guardian*, 7 January 1915.
4. ibid.
5. Quoted in hmsformidable.org.
6. Admiralty file, case 11166, NA.
7. Quoted in *Exeter Express and Echo*, February 5, 2010.
8. *Belfast Evening Telegraph*, 26 January 1916.
9. *Wanganui Chronicle*, 6 January 1915.
10. *Brixham Western Guardian*, 7 January 1915.
11. ibid.
12. *Belfast Evening Telegraph*, 9 January 1915.
13. *Brixham Western Guardian*, 7 January 1915.
14. ibid.
15. ibid.
16. ibid.
17. ibid.
18. ibid.

Chapter 7, Two Dogs and Some Funerals
1. Quoted in hmsformidable.org.
2. *Daily Chronicle*, 5 January 1915.
3. A.P. Terhune, *The New Complete Airedale Terrier*.
4. Quoted in hmsformidable.org.
5. *Western Morning News* of January 1915, reprinted in the 19 October 1982 edition.
6. *Crewe Chronicle*, 9 January 1915.
7. *Crewe Guardian*, 8 January 1915.
8. *Crewe Chronicle*, 9 January 1915.
9. ibid.

10. ibid.
11. *Crewe Guardian*, 8 January 1915.
12. *Crewe Chronicle*, 9 January 1915.
13. Admiralty file, case 11166, NA.
14. *The Western Gazette*, 8 January 1915.
15. *Wanganui Chronicle*, 6 January 1915.
16. *Sydney Morning Herald*, 12 February 1915.
17. *King Hall connections*, letters from HMS *Southampton*, online.
18. *Brixham Western Guardian*, 7 January 1915.
19. Quoted in *Through Cloud and Sunshine*, SFP Little, Brixham Heritage Museum, 2008.
20. ibid.

Chapter 8, Après le Déluge
1. Lord Crewe, statement to the House of Lords, 7 January 1915, quoted in the *Darlington and Stockton Times*, 9 January, 1915.

Chapter 9, To Be an Admiral
1. Marder, *From the Dreadnought to Scapa Flow, vol 2.*
2. ibid.
3. ibid.

Chapter 10, The Culprit
1. *Nelson Evening Mail*, 4 January 1915.
2. 'Lambda', *Naval Review*, 1939.
3. A.J. Marder, *From the Dreadnought to Scapa Flow, vol 2*, OUP, 1965.
4. D. de Chair, *The Sea is Strong*, Harrap & Co, 1961.
5. Admiralty Records, NA.
6. Jellicoe to Jackson, 29 April 1916, Jackson papers, Museum of the Royal Navy, Portsmouth.
7. T. Wilson Ross, 'A Naval Encounter', *Naval Historical Review*, 1975.
8. Letter, Churchill Archive Centre (CAC), Churchill College, Cambridge.
9. Letter, 9 December 1913, CAC.
10. Letter, CAC.
11. Asquith MSS.
12. Marder, *From the Dreadnought to Scapa Flow, vol 1.*
13. L. Bayly, *Pull Together*, G. Harrap & Co, 1939.

14. Richmond, diary, 4 January 1915, National Maritime Museum (NMM).
15. Quoted in Marder, *From the Dreadnought to Scapa Flow*, vol 2.
16. Letter, CAC.
17. Letter, CAC.
18. Letter, 13 January 1915, CAC.
19. Churchill MSS, CAC.
20. Quoted in M. Potts & T. Marks, *Before the Bells have Faded*, Naval and Military Press, 2004.
21. *King-Hall Connections*, online, letter, 11 January 1915.
22. Hamilton papers, NMM.
23. Quoted in M. Gilbert, *Winston S. Churchill vol III*, Heinemann Books, 1973.
24. Bayly, *Pull Together*.
25. ibid.
26. ibid.
27. Hansard, 1915.
28. ibid.

Chapter 11, The Admiral and the Admiralty

1. W. Graham Greene to Bayly, 11 January 1915, NA.
2. ibid.
3. ibid.
4. ibid.
5. ibid.
6. Bayly to Admiralty, 13 January 1915, NA.
7. ibid.
8. W. Graham Greene to Bayly, 10 February 1915, NA.
9. ibid.
10. Unsigned, undated letter, CAC.
11. Bayly, *Pull Together*.
12. Bayly to Secretary of the Admiralty, 17 March 1919, NA.
13. Bayly, *Pull Together*.
14. Bayly to Admiralty, 1 May 1919, NA.
15. ibid.
16. ibid.
17. Admiralty file NL15831/19, NA.
18. ibid.
19. Bayly to Secretary of the Admiralty, 28 May 1919, NA.
20. Letter, 21 July 1935, CAC.
21. Letter, 23 July 1935, CAC.

Chapter 12, The Captain Went Down with the Ship
1. T. Hughes, *Tom Brown's Schooldays*, Macmillan, 1857.
2. Quoted in M. Bostridge, *The Fateful Year*, Viking, 2014.
3. K. Tyler-Lewis, *The Lost Men, Bloomsbury*, 2006.
4. Quoted in M. Pugh, *We Danced all Night*, Vintage, 2009.
5. Quoted in Mark of Whitstable, *Gospel Chivalry*, Gracewing, 2006.
6 P. Howarth, *Play up and play the game*, Eyre Methuen, 1973.
7. R. Winder, *The Little Wonder*, Bloomsbury 2013.
8. ibid.
9. S. Sassoon, *Counter attack and other poems*, E.P. Dutton & Co, 1918.
10. L. Bayly, *Pull Together*, G. Harrap & Co, 1939.
11. *The Times*, 9 April 1852.
12. S. Spignesi, *The Titanic for Dummies*, John Wiley & Sons, 2012.
13. R. Ballard, *The Discovery of the Titanic*, Hodder and Stoughton, 1987.
14. Quoted in the *Guardian*, 20 January 2012.
15. W. Lord, *The Night Lives On*, William Morrow and Company, 1986.
16. *Belfast Evening Telegraph*, January 9 1915.

Chapter 13, Pro Patria
1. *The Independent*, Lord Colyton obituary, 8 January 1996.
2. Quoted in Potts and Marks, *Before the Bells have Faded*.
3. *Surrey Advertiser*, 16 January 1915.
4. *Herald*, 16 January 1915.
5. *Western Time*, 13 January 1915.
6. Duff papers, diary, 8 January 1915, NMM.
7. Potts and Marks, *Before the Bells have Faded*.
8. J. Corbett, *History of the Great War, Naval Operation*, Longmans Green and Co, 1920.

Chapter 14, Patriotism and Propaganda
1. *Quoted in the Wanganui Chronicle*, 6 January 1915.
2. *Sydney Morning Herald*, 12 February 1915.
3. Quoted in *New York Times*, 9 January 1915.
4. *Daily Mail*, 4 January 1915.
5. Quoted in Potts and Marks, *Before the Bells have Faded*.
6. Quoted ibid.
7. Guild hall, Lyme Regis.
8. Quoted in the *Evening News* of New Zealand, 8 May 1915.
9. Produced by *Topical Budget News*, 1915.

10. *London Gazette*, 1 September 1914.
11. L. Knight, *The Diaries of Beatrice Webb*, Virago, 2002.
12. E. Parrot, *The Children's Story of the War*, T. Nelson and Sons, 1916.

Chapter 15, The Dogs of War
1. *Daily Express*, 28 November 2013.
2. E.H. Richardson, *British War Dogs, their training and psychology*, Skeffington and Sons, 1920.
3. C. Miskow, *A History of the Airedale Terrier*, undated online essay.
4. Blog, Mary Evans Picture Library.
5. Richardson, *British War Dogs*.

Chapter 16, Memorials to the Fallen
1. Quoted in *The Concise Oxford Dictionary of Quotations*, OUP, 1964.

Chapter 17, Those Left Behind
1. *The Times*, 12 July 1915.
2. Matthew 26:11.
3. Quoted in P. Higginbottom, workhouses.org.uk, 2011.
4. *Daily Telegraph*, 6 January 1914.
5. *Herald*, 16 January 1915.
6. *Darlington and Stockton Times*, 16 January 1915.
7. A. Carew, *The Lower Deck in the British Navy 1900-1936*, Manchester University Press, 1981.
8. *Hansard*, May 1917.
9. *What is our task? To make Britain a fit country for heroes to live in.* David Lloyd George, speech at Wolverhampton, 23 November 1918.

Chapter 18, Postscript
1. Quoted in Little, *Through Cloud and Sunshine*.
2. See Chapter 10.

Appendix 1, The 'Lassie Legend'
1. N. Clarke, *Shipwreck Guide to Dorset and South Devon*, Nigel J. Clarke Publications, 2008.

Appendix 5, Propaganda and the Defence of the Realm Act – part two
1. Quoted in A. Hochschild, *To end all wars*, Pan Books, 2002.

Select Bibliography

Books

Ballard, R., *The Discovery of the Titanic*, Hodder and Stoughton, 1987.

Bayly, L., *Pull Together*, G. Harrap & Co, 1939.

Bostridge, M., *The Fateful Year*, Viking, 2014.

Carew, A., *The Lower Deck in the British Navy 1900–1936*, Manchester University Press, 1981.

Clarke, N. *Shipwreck Guide to Dorset and South Devon*, Nigel J. Clarke Publications, 2008.

Corbett, Sir J., *History of the Great War, Naval Operations*, Longmans Green and Co, 1920.

De Chair, D., *The Sea is Strong*, Harrap & Co, 1961.

Gilbert, M., *Winston S. Churchill vol III*, Heinemann Books, 2002.

Hochschild, A., *To end all wars*, Pan Books.

Howarth, P., *Play up and play the game*, Eyre Methuen, 1973.

Hughes, T., *Tom Brown's Schooldays*, Macmillan, 1857.

Jane, F.T., *Jane's Fighting Ships of World War I*, Jane's Publishing Company, 1919.

Knight, L., *The Diaries of Beatrice Webb*, Virago, 2002.

Little, S.F.P., *Through Cloud and Sunshine, Brixham in the Great War*, Brixham Heritage Museum, 2008.

Lord, W., *The Night Lives on*, William Morrow and Co, 1986.

Marder, A.J., *From the Dreadnought to Scapa Flow, vols 1 &2*, OUP, 1965.

McLaughlin, R., *The Escape of the Goeben*, Seeley Service, 1974.

Parrot, E., *The Children's Story of the War*, T. Nelson and Sons, 1916.

Penrose Fitzgerald, C.C., *From Steam to Sail*, E. Arnold, 1922.

Potts, M. and Marks, T., *Before the Bells have Faded*, Naval and Military Press, 2004.

Pugh, M., *We Danced All Night*, Vintage, 2009.

Richardson, E.H., *British War Dogs, their training and psychology*, Skeffington and Sons, 1920.

Sassoon, S., *Counter attack and other poems*, E.P. Dutton & Co, 1918.

Spignesi, S., *The Titanic for Dummies*, John Wiley & Sons, 2012.

Treherne, A.P., *The New Complete Airedale Terrier* (in *The 20th Century Dog*, Grant Richards, 1904).

Tuchman, B., *The Proud Tower*, Hamish Hamilton, 1966.

Tucker, J.S., *Admiral the Right Hon The Earl of St Vincent GCB&C, Memoirs*, Richard Bentley, 1844.

Tyler-Lewis, K., *The Lost Men*, Bloomsbury, 2006.

Whitstable, Mark of, *Gospel Chivalry*, Gracewing, 2006.
Winder, R., *The Little Wonder*, Bloomsbury, 2013.
Wragg, D., *Royal Navy Handbook 1914-18*, Sutton Publishing, 2006.

Online sources
Burton Bradstock online
Dreadnoughtproject.org
Hmsformidable.org (which is actually a site devoted to the Second World War aircraft carrier of the same name)
Mary Evans Picture Library blog
Naval-history.net
Scarborough Maritime Heritage Centre
Wikipedia.org

Newspapers and magazines
Belfast Evening Telegraph
Brixham Western Guardian
Crewe Chronicle
Crewe Guardian
Daily Chronicle
Daily Express
Daily Mail
Daily Telegraph
Darlington and Stockton Times
Evening News, NZ
Exeter Express and Echo
Guardian
Herald
Independent
London Gazette
Naval Historical Review
Naval Review
Nelson Evening Mail, NZ
New York Times
New York Tribune
South Devon Herald Express
Surrey Advertiser
Sydney Morning Herald
Wanganui Chronicle, NZ
Western Gazette
Western Times

Index

Page references in *italic* indicate illustrations.

223

224

Enfield Lock 211
Etaples 161
Eton 23, 124-8, 135, 136
Evan-Thomas, Hugh 185
Ewhurst, Surrey 139
Excellent, HMS 26, 136

Falmouth 20
Fawkes, W. 73
Feldon, W. 72, 73
film 157-8
First World War
    America's entry 117
    British naval casualties 146-7
    British volunteers before
        conscription 168
    censorship 154-5, 210-11
    dogs in *see* dogs
    as last stand of chivalry 203-4
    marriageable generation of men
        wiped out by 186
    outbreak 18-20
    propaganda 155-8, 209-12
    remembrance movement 168-73
    shell shock 194
    total fatalities 147
    Turkey's entry into 29
    'war babies' 158
    war widows' pensions 177-80
    Western Front *see* Western Front
    and women's employment 183-4
Fisher, Jack (Able Seaman) 55,
    195-6
Fisher, John Arbuthnot 'Jackie', 1st
    Baron 4, 17-18, 39-40, 96, 200
    and Arbuthnot 26
    and Bayly 105, 106, 116
    and Churchill 4, 39-40, 105, 106,
        107
    and flotilla defence 40
    'nucleus crew' concept 32
flotation collars 53, 58, 59, 80-81
flotilla defence 40
Foad, William John 142
football 126-7

Force C 41
Ford, Ford Madox 155
Forde, Florrie 192
Forest 9
Formidable, HMS, aircraft carrier 191
Formidable, HMS, battleship 13-20,
    31-2, *97*, *100*
    aftermath of disaster 199-201
    auxiliary boats 45, 47, 49, 50-51,
        59, 64-6, 71
    badge/crest 63, 152
    and Bayly 36
    blame between Admiralty and
        Bayly for loss of 104-8, 112-20,
        200-201
    captains before Loxley 212-13
    casualties 52, 53-4, 63-4, 70-74,
        75-81, 148-9
    Churchill questioned in House of
        Commons on loss of 109-10
    communal grave, Lyme Regis *98*
    crew 32, 44, 48-52, 53-8
    death notifications to next of kin
        133-4
    dependents 174-86
    Dixon painting 14
    families left behind 133-4, 137,
        174-86
    guns 14, 30
    lifebelt washed up on Dutch coast
        81-2
    Loxley's posting to 29-30
    married men 174-5
    masons lost with 145
    medical department 50, 142
    with Mediterranean Fleet 14-15,
        16
    memorial service, Brixham 75-6
    memorial service, Chatham 134
    memorial service, Crewe 76-8
    memorial service, Lyme Regis
        72-4, *98*
    memorials raised to the fallen
        135-45, 167-73

INDEX

Wellington, Arthur Wellesley, 1st
    Duke of 167
Wells, H.G. 155
Wemyss, Rosslyn, 1st Baron Wester
    Wemyss 120
West, C.W. 146
Western Front 1, 76, 91, 125, 135,
    145, 153-4, 158, 178, 210
  dogs on 159, 161-2
Westminster Gazette 83-4
Wheatley, Eddison ('Eddie') 59, 67,
    195
Where's Master? 136, 156
White Star Line 146
Wilhelm II, Kaiser 146
Williams, Captain 8
Williams, Henry James 'Harry' 192,
    193
Williams, Valentine 210
Wilson, Sir Arthur Knyvet 38,
    39

Wilson, George W. 57, 63, 69, 194,
    195
Wilson, Woodrow 146
Wisden 127, 128
women's curfews 211-12
women's employment 183-4
women's movement 181-2
Woods, Roland Walter 139
Wordsworth, John 8
Wordsworth, William 8
World Wars *see* First World War;
    Second World War
Wright, Ada 185
Wright, Wesley H. 185
Wyke Regis 8
Wynne, Trethowan Campbell
    Trevredyn 197

Yonge, Charlotte M.: *The Heir of
    Redcliffe* 123
Ypres, Battle of 2